NAHC
Wild Game Cookbook

Edited by
Mike Vail

North American Hunting Club
Minneapolis, Minnesota

Acknowledgements

We would like to thank the following for their help:

NAHC Members, for sending us those delicious, original wild game recipes that serve as the foundation of the 1996 NAHC Wild Game Cookbook. These recipes – recommended by your fellow NAHC Members – are certain to delight.

Life Member, Chef John Schumacher, of Schumachers Historic European Hotel and Restaurant in New Prague, Minnesota for his expert game cooking advice and recipes.

Lawry's Foods, for their delicious game recipe contributions.

NAHC staff members, for their diligence, patience and hard work in seeing to the preparation off a useful and readable cookbook of which the NAHC's members can be proud. They include Marketing Manager of Books Cal Franklin and Project Coordinator Sherry Bania.

Book Design by Zins Design Studio
Illustrations by Brian Jensen

Please address reprint requests
and orders for additional cookbooks to:
NAHC Cookbook Editor
P.O. Box 3401
Minneapolis, MN 55343

Library of Congress Catalog Card Number 84-649847
ISBN 0-914697-65-X
Copyright 1996, North American Hunting Club

Dedication

After all these years of producing our popular <u>NAHC Wild Game Cookbook</u>, we've failed to recognize one particular group for its contribution to the success of this annual publication: The NAHC Staff.

You won't find a more dedicated group of hunters anywhere! We put in long hours to create the Club's great magazine — *North American Hunter*. We also spend a lot of time working to provide Members with all the benefits they deserve and look forward to, the benefits of membership in America's leading hunting organization.

Every year, as we start work on the annual <u>Wild Game Cookbook</u>, we read through hundreds of recipes that are sent to us by Members of the Club. And it's a tough job to separate the best so they can be included in the cookbook — they all sound so good.

This year, as we were sorting through Member recipes, a thought struck us: what about all the tried and true recipes enjoyed by our own Hunting Club staff? Who would have better recipes? After all, even though we spend a lot of time taking care of Club business, most of us somehow find time to get out in the field in the quest of our favorite game.

So, I sent out a memo. Each staff member was asked for a favorite wild game recipe. And we got a bunch. In this edition of the <u>NAHC Wild Game Cookbook</u>, you'll find some of our favorites.

This edition is dedicated to the Club staff, without whom this would all be impossible.

Mike Vail,
Editor

Contents

Introduction 7

Staff Recipes 9

Venison 29

Big Game 93

Small Game 129

Game Birds 139

Waterfowl 155

Lawry's Wild Game Recipes 171

Index 187

Cookbook Abbreviations

tsp. = teaspoon
T. = tablespoon
pt. = pint
oz. = ounce
pkg. = package
qt. = quart

Measurement Conversions

1 pinch = less than ⅛ tsp.
1 T. = 3 tsp.
2 T. = 1 oz.
4 T. = ¼ cup
5 T + 1 tsp. = ⅓ cup
8 T. = ½ cup
16 T. = 1 cup

1 cup = 8 oz.
1 pint = 16 oz.
1 quart = 32 oz.
1 gallon = 128 oz.

1 cup = ½ pint
2 cups = 1 pint
4 cups = 1 quart
2 pints = 1 quart
4 pints = ½ gallon
8 pints = 1 gallon
4 quarts = 1 gallon
8 gallons = 1 bushel

Introduction

It was the opening line in an early *1996* "View From Here" in *North American Hunter* magazine. I wrote "Folks never let me forget what a great job I have."

That comment held true then and

Bill Miller

it still holds true today. As Executive Director of the North American Hunting Club and Editor of *North American Hunter* magazine I do have a great job. And NAHC Members, rightly so, never let me forget it! It's because of Members like you that my job is so great! If there's any other organization of people so willing to lend a hand to help their fellow Members enjoy hunting success more, I sure don't know about it! In fact, I'm certain such an organization does not exist, because NAHC Members represent the epitome of helpfulness and sports-person-ship.

That attitude comes through in the coming together of Members at NAHC events like Jamborees and Club Days. It's certainly evident in the popularity of interactive benefits like Swap Hunts, Discounts and Meeting Place. And we try to share more stories each and every year of Members who have distinguished themselves by presenting a truly positive image for us all to the non-hunting public.

Even with all of those great examples, I don't think there is a better representation of North American Hunting Club's Members' willingness to share the joys of hunting than the annual *NAHC Wild Game Cookbook*. For well over a decade now, the NAHC has been able to compile one great cookbook after another based for the most part on recipes, field care, butchering, storage and kitchen tips submitted by NAHC Members. When you think about the thousands of recipes and tips which this has covered, it really hits home how generous NAHC Members have been and continue to be. We don't take the credit for this, it's Members sharing with Members. The NAHC is just the clearing house for all of this great knowledge and advice.

Well, this year's *NAHC Wild Game Cookbook* is no different in that respect. We've included hundreds of new recipes and tips submitted by NAHC Members. On the other hand, we wanted to give something back to all of you; something that would say thank you for all of your support season after season and year after year. So, this edition of the *NAHC Wild Game Cookbook* includes a section of favorite recipes and tips provided by the staff of the North American Hunting Club.

Some of these recipes are home spun favorites that the folks who work here have enjoyed since childhood. Others are recipes we've gathered from hunting camps scattered across the breadth of North America. The tips are ones we've come to trust based upon trying them ourselves in the woods and in our kitchens at home. We've hunted the game, we've made these recipes and our families have enjoyed the results.

Though we owe you a lot more for your participation and generosity over the years, we hope that by trying our favorite wild game recipes you enjoy your hunting a little bit more this year and in the seasons ahead.

If that is indeed the result of this cookbook, then we have climbed another rung higher toward the most basic goal of the North American Hunting Club. We'll have helped to enhance your hunting success, enjoyment, safety and ethics. After all, that's what we're here to do!

Enjoy and eat hardy!

Bill

Bill Miller
Executive Director

Staff Recipes

Bill Miller's Favorite Ways To Eat Wild Game

I like steaks! It doesn't matter whether it's whitetail, an elk, a mulie, a moose, a musk ox, a caribou, or a nilgai. On those occasions where I'm asked what my favorite meal is, I don't have to hesitate one second to answer! I like a medium-rare wild game steak grilled outdoors over charcoal. Better make that two or three if I'm hungry!

The truth is I've come to like wild game steaks cooked at home so much, I'm usually disappointed these days when I order a steak in a restaurant. It just doesn't seem to have any flavor compared to steaks and chops cut from critters that have to use their wits and their physical stamina to survive every day of their lives. And besides the exquisite flavor there is an intrinsic pride in the self-sufficiency of having hunted, killed, field dressed, cared for and cooked the meat which feeds you and your family and friends.

Along with my steaks I like a big baked potato loaded with sour cream, real butter and onion chives cut fresh from the garden. Along side that give me at least a couple of ears of sweet corn so fresh and so succulent it squirts sugary juices on my chin with every bite. It too is covered in butter with a generous seasoning of salt.

The perfect salad for this feast is marinated tomatoes and onions. All you do is slice up a couple of tomatoes and a couple of big red onions both fresh from the garden. Place them in a deep bowl and pour an entire bottle of your favorite vinegar and oil Italian salad dressing over the top. Let them sit for at least a couple of hours, sloshing the bowl around once or twice to be sure the dressing gets to everything. You can even let this sit over night; that makes it even better!

Dessert can only be one thing! My wife's special peach cobbler recipe with a big dollop of good vanilla ice cream on top. I'd share that recipe, too, but you might be disappointed. I've tried the peach cobbler of those who've tried to duplicate my wife's and I've always been disappointed.

The drink to go with this fabulous meal would depend on my mood. In the summertime it might be ice tea, lemonade or ice cold milk. If I'm in the mood for an adult beverage, a good full-bodied beer would be great. If I'm feeling sophisticated, there'd be a bottle of good cabernet on the table. Were you to put me in front of a firing squad, this is no doubt the meal you'd be serving as my last!

Bill Miller's Wild Game Steak Recipe

(It Just Doesn't Get Any Easier Than This!)

4-6 venison, elk, moose or caribou
  steaks completely thawed with all
  fat and silver skin trimmed away
butter or butter substitute, melted
  or in the spray bottle
garlic salt

Worcestershire Sauce
fresh ground black pepper
lemon pepper
Tabasco Sauce (optional)
cayenne Pepper (optional)

Spread the steaks out on a large plate. Spray or brush on a generous amount of butter. Give each steak a splash of Worcestershire. Season to your liking with the garlic salt, black pepper and lemon pepper. If you want more spice use the Tabasco or cayenne. Flip the steaks over and repeat on the other side. Then let them rest in the juices for at least 15 minutes; an hour is better.

Get a medium hot fire going on the charcoal or gas grill. Slap the steaks on the grate and hit 'em once more with the butter. For the way my butcher cuts the steaks, I grill from five to six minutes aside. This leaves the meat flame kissed on the outside and nice and pink, but hot in the center.

It's even more critical with wild game than it is with beef that you do not overcook the steaks. Game steaks dry out and toughen very quickly because all of the fat is removed. Don't worry about serving it to folks who claim they don't like wild game meat or don't like lightly cooked steaks. This is the only kind of meat and the only way we cook steaks at our house. We've served them this way for many dinner parties and have only received raves. And I watch closely to make sure everyone really enjoys it. If they don't they probably won't be invited back anyway because they ain't the sort of folks we'd want to hang around with.

Enjoy red meat!

Serves: 4-6

Bill Miller
NAHC Staff

Sweet & Sour Snow Goose

1 med. goose
¾ cup orange marmalade
¼ cup vinegar
⅛ cup lemon juice
1 tsp. salt
1 tsp. pepper
¼ tsp. dry mustard

Sauce

1 T. butter
½ tsp. Worcestershire sauce
½ tsp. ketchup
¼ tsp. lemon juice
1 T. currant jelly

Steve Burke

Soak goose in saltwater for 2 hours. Mix next 6 ingredients and pour over drained goose in small casserole. Cover and cook for 1 hour at 325 degrees, basting as needed. Uncover and cook for 30 minutes longer, basting often. Remove goose with a slotted spoon. Combine sauce and ingredients and pour over goose at serving time.

Serves: 4

Steve Burke
NAHC Staff

Russ's Whiskey Wild Turkey

Russ Nolan

 6 turkey breasts, sliced
   salt
   pepper (white or black)
¾ cup flour
½ cup butter or margarine
 1 onion (sliced)
¾ cup of favorite whiskey

Season turkey breasts with salt and pepper, roll in flour, fry in butter over medium-high heat. Add whiskey and onion. when breasts are golden brown on both sides, lower heat and cover. Continue cooking until meat falls apart when turned with fork.

Excellent when served with wild rice.

Serves: 10-12

Russ Nolan
NAHC Staff

13

Gregg Gutschow

Pheasant in Mushroom Sauce

2 pheasants, breasts and legs
1 can cream of mushroom soup
½ cup sour cream
¼ cup milk
2 T. sherry
1 tsp. salt
½ tsp. pepper
½ cup flour
¼ cup vegetable oil
1 medium onion, coarsely chopped
8 oz. fresh, whole mushrooms

Preheat oven to 300 degrees. Blend soup, sour cream, milk and sherry; set aside. In large resealable plastic bag, combine salt, pepper and flour. Add pheasant and coat.

In Dutch oven, heat oil over medium high heat. Brown pheasant. Add mushrooms, onion and soup mixture. Cover and bake for 1½ - 2 hours.

Serves: 4

Gregg Gutschow
NAHC Staff

Pitica

Meat

3-5 lbs. venison roast
  1 large yellow onion, coarsely chopped
  2 eggs
    salt and pepper to
      taste
    milk

Roast venison until done. Grind up with onion. Add salt, pepper and eggs. Add enough milk to hold meat together.

Dough

  ¼ cup sugar
  2 cups water
  2 eggs
  ½ cup melted shortening
  2 pkg. dry yeast
  6 cups flour
  1 tsp. salt

Teri Glover

Mix all ingredients together and let dough rise. Roll out dough, cut into circles 4" in diameter. Put small amount of meat onto dough and fold in half. Seal edges with milk. Deep fry until dough is golden brown.

These freeze well and can be reheated in oven or microwave.

Yields: 24 servings

Teri Glover
NAHC Staff

15

Doug McDougal, 2nd from left, and friends

Pheasant Nibblers

4-6 pheasant breasts, cut into
        1" pieces
      Italian salad dressing
1 lb. bacon, cut into 2" strips

Marinate pheasant in Italian dressing
for 12 hours or more. Wrap bacon
around each pheasant piece and
secure with a toothpick. Grill nibblers
over a hot fire or under broiler until
the bacon starts to get crispy (watch
for flame-ups from the Italian dressing
oil).

Serves: 8-12

Doug McDougal
NAHC Staff

Pheasant Diane

6 pheasant breasts
    melted butter
    lemon pepper (to taste)
    garlic salt (to taste)
    spinach or egg noodles
    Parmesan cheese

Place pheasant breasts in a glass dish so
that they are not touching. Brush with
melted butter. Season with lemon pepper and garlic salt. Bake at 350 degrees
for 18-20 minutes (do not over cook).
Place on cooked noodles and sprinkle
with salt, pepper and Parmesan cheese.

Serves: 4

Doug McDougal
NAHC Staff

Dan's Delicious Pheasant

1 pheasant
½ cup flour
1 tsp. salt
1 tsp. pepper
2 T. cooking oil
1 small onion, chopped
1 cup sour cream
1 can cream of
    mushroom soup

Cut pheasant into large pieces, dip in flour, salt and pepper. Heat oil in frying pan and brown pheasant. Remove pheasant and fry onion in same pan. Mix in sour cream and cream of mushroom soup. Place pheasant in baking dish and pour sauce over it. Bake at 350 degrees for approximately 2 hours.

Serves: 2

Dan Kennedy
NAHC Staff

Dan Kennedy

Dan's Primo Duck and Goose

duck or goose breasts, cut into 1" cubes
bacon, cut strips in half
Italian salad dressing (enough to cover meat)

Marinate duck or goose cubes in Italian dressing for 24 hours. Wrap each cube in uncooked bacon strip. Put on skewers and grill on medium to medium high heat for 10-12 minutes or until bacon is done. This recipe promises to become a favorite.

Yields: 12-14 pieces per duck

Dan Kennedy
NAHC Staff

17

Dave's Famous Venison Kabobs

2 lb. venison chunks
2 large onions, quartered and
  separated

2 green peppers, cut into 1" squares
2 red potatoes, quartered
1 can pineapple chunks

Marinade

¾ cup salad oil
⅓ cup soy sauce
⅓ cup lemon juice
½ tsp. garlic salt
½ tsp. pepper
½ tsp. dry mustard

Mix marinade in a shallow pan. Add venison and marinate for 3-4 hours in refrigerator. Place on skewers along with onions, peppers, potatoes and pineapple. Grill.

Serves: 8

Jeff Boehler
NAHC Staff

Bagged Venison Roast

3 lb. venison roast
2 T. flour
1 bay leaf
8 whole cloves
1 medium onion
1 cup dry red wine
1 6" x 10" baking bag

Shake flour and venison in bag, turning to coat. Add remaining ingredients. Close bag with nylon tie and slash six ½" slits in top of bag to let steam escape. Insert a meat thermometer through bag into thickest part of roast. Bake at 325 degrees for 1½ - 2 hours or until temperature reaches 180 degrees.

Serves: 8

Jeff Boehler
NAHC Staff

Jeff Boehler

Gramma Larson's Golden Goose

goose
salt and pepper
sauerkraut
bacon strips
wine

Rub salt and pepper inside the clean cavity of a goose. Fill cavity with sauerkraut. Place foil in the bottom of a roaster with enough overlap to allow for covering the bird. Cover the goose breasts with bacon strips. Pull foil around the bird and seal.

Bake at 350 degrees for 5-7 hours, depending on the size of the bird. Bake until drumstick meat is tender. Uncover the goose for the last hour of baking and baste with wine. Gramma uses homemade rhubarb wine but a red wine would work just fine.

Serves: 8-12 (depending on size of goose)

Jeff Boehler
NAHC Staff

Instant Gander

2 lbs. wild goose
instant coffee granules or cold coffee grounds
bacon strips

Cut goose meat into strips. Dip in water and then coffee granules or grounds. Wrap in bacon and hold together with toothpicks. Broil over coals. Sounds weird but tastes great!

Serves: 4

Jeff Boehler
NAHC Staff

Upper Lightning Roasted Duck

1 whole picked duck
salt and pepper
1 orange, quartered

1 apple, quartered
1 onion, quartered

Salt and pepper clean cavity of duck. Put oranges, apples and onions in cavity. Bake at 425 degrees for about 2 - 2½ hours. We bake it in a hot oven to keep it a little crispy on the outside and moist on the inside.

Serves: 4

Jeff Boehler
NAHC Staff

Wild Game Barbecue Sauce

2½ cups ketchup
2½ T. Worcestershire sauce
few grains cayenne pepper
½ tsp. chili powder

½ cup sugar
½ clove garlic or ½ tsp. liquid garlic
2 tsp. liquid smoke

Combine ingredients. Bring to a boil. Store in refrigerator. Excellent on elk, deer and big horn sheep.

Connie Schlundt
NAHC Staff

Venison Shish Kabobs

1 lb. venison, cut into 1" x 1" x ½" cubes
1 large onion
1 potato
1 large green pepper
24 cherry tomatoes
24 fresh mushrooms
    Italian salad
        dressing

Michael Faw

Marinate venison cubes for several hours in Italian dressing. When ready to grill, cut other ingredients into large bitesized pieces and alternate ingredients on skewers (best to place onion and green pepper chunks next to venison cubes and slice potatoes thinner since they cook slower). Brush kabobs with dressing.

Preheat grill on low heat and place skewers on the grill. Turn frequently and watch onions, green pepper and tomatoes closely because they burn easily.

When cooked to taste, sprinkle with salt and pepper and remove from skewers or serve as is and let diner remove. Serve with fresh baked croissants and Merlot wine.

Serves: 2-4

Michael Faw
NAHC Staff

Michael Faw

Groundhawg Bake

- 1 medium-to-large groundhog
- 1 cup white vinegar
- 1 onion, quartered
- 1 tsp. black pepper
- 2 large potatoes, quartered
- 2 carrots, in bitesized chunks

Skin and clean groundhog (be careful when touching glands on insides of legs). Soak groundhog overnight in solution of 1 cup white vinegar to 1 gallon water.

Remove groundhog and place in large pot with onion and black pepper. Boil until tender, approximately 2 hours. Remove from pot and place in roasting pan with potatoes and carrots. Sprinkle with your favorite seasoning, cover dish with foil and roast at 350 degrees for 2 hours or until browned.

Serves: 2-4

Michael Faw
NAHC Staff

Grouse and Wild Rice Salad

Tracy Wright

- 3 cups cut up cooked grouse
- ⅔ cup mayonnaise
- ⅓ cup milk
- 2 T. lemon juice
- ¼ tsp. dried tarragon, crumbled
- 3 cups cooked wild rice
- ⅓ cup finely sliced green onion
- 1 8-oz. can sliced water chestnuts, drained
- ½ tsp. salt
- ⅛ tsp. pepper
- 1 cup seedless green grapes, halved
- 1 cup salted cashews

Blend mayonnaise, milk, lemon juice and tarragon and set aside. Combine grouse, wild rice, green onions, water chestnuts, salt and pepper in large bowl. Stir in mayonnaise mixture until blended. Cover and refrigerate for 2-3 hours. Fold in grapes and cashews just before serving.

Yields: 8 1-cup servings

Tracy Wright
NAHC Staff

23

Caribou Tamales

Filling

1 lb. ground caribou
2 T. butter
½ cup chopped onion
¼ cup chopped green pepper
⅛ tsp. ground pepper
1 16-oz. can pork and beans

1 16-oz. can dark red kidney
  beans, drained
1 16-oz. can tomatoes, drained
1 tsp. salt
2 tsp. chili powder

Masa dough

1 cup shortening
2 tsp. chili powder
1¾ cup water
2½ cups Masa harina
1 tsp. salt
24 6" aluminum foil squares

For filling, melt butter in large pan. Saute onion and green pepper until tender. Add ground caribou and brown. Add remaining ingredients. Simmer covered for 15 minutes.

For Masa dough, beat shortening until fluffy. Add chili powder, water, Masa and salt. Beat until light and fluffy - until a spoonful floats on warm water.

To assemble, divide Masa dough into 24 equal portions. Place each portion on a foil square. Spread each to form a 4" square, keeping one side even with one edge of foil. Top with 1-2 tablespoons filling; roll up like a jelly roll starting with the side of the dough even with the edge of the foil. Fold one end up, sealing well (leave the other end open).

Stack tamales open end up on rack above gently boiling water (I use a canner). Cover and cook about 1 hour until Masa dough does not stick to foil. Serve warm with fresh salsa.

Serves: 8-12

Beth Metzen
NAHC Staff

Grilled Grouse

4 boneless breast halves from 2 grouse
1 cup onions, minced
1 clove fresh garlic, minced
1 T. seasoning salt
8 strips bacon

Flatten each of 4 breast halves with mallet or back of large knife. Spread with mixture of chopped onions and pinch of fresh garlic. Fold breast to cover onion and garlic mixture. Sprinkle with seasoning salt. Wrap two strips of bacon around each grouse breast half to cover completely. Secure with toothpicks. Grill over medium coals until cooked through.

Serves: 4

Tracy Wright
NAHC Staff

Cherokee Casserole

1½ lbs. ground elk or deer
1 T. salad or olive oil
¾ cup finely chopped onions
1½ tsp. salt
⅛ tsp. garlic powder
⅛ tsp. thyme
⅛ tsp. oregano
dash of pepper

½ small bay leaf
2 8-oz. cans tomato sauce or
    16-oz. can tomatoes
1 can cream of mushroom soup
1 cup instant rice, cooked
3 stuffed olives, sliced
2-3 slices cheese, cut in ½" strips

Brown meat in oil over high heat. Add onions and cook until tender. Stir in remaining ingredients in order given, except cheese. Bring to a boil, reduce heat, and simmer for 5 minutes, stirring occasionally. Discard bay leaf. Arrange a layer of cheese over top. Simmer until cheese melts. Garnish with additional sliced stuffed olives, if desired.

Serves: 4-6

Connie Schlundt
NAHC Staff

Grilled Quail with Hot Sauce

8 quail, cleaned and boned	¼ tsp. cumin seeds, toasted
2 dried jalapeno chilies, seeded	¼ tsp. coriander seeds, toasted
2 dried ancho chilies, and seeded	½ cup toasted whole almonds, chopped
½ cup chopped onion	4 T. vegetable oil
1 ripe tomato	4 T. olive oil
2 garlic cloves, minced	4 tsp. whitewine vinegar
¼ cup fresh coriander sprigs	2 T. pure maple syrup
½ cup orange juice	1 tsp. coarse salt
1 cup water	
¼ tsp. cinnamon	

First, make the sauce. In a heavy saucepan, cook the dried chilies over medium heat for 1 minute, turning continuously (be careful not to burn them) and set aside. Put the onion, tomato and garlic into the pan and cook at a medium-high heat, stirring frequently until the tomato skin is blistered and the onion and garlic are light brown. Add the chilies back into the pan along with the coriander sprigs, orange juice, water, cinnamon, cumin seeds and coriander seeds. Bring to a boil, and simmer the mixture, stirring, for 10-15 minutes, or until thickened.

Transfer to a blender and add the almonds, both oils, vinegar, syrup and salt. Puree until smooth. Put half of the sauce in the refrigerator until needed.

Cut the skin on the back of the quails so they lie flat. Place the quail in resealable plastic bags, and pour the remaining sauce over the quail, coating them well. Seal the bags, press out any excess air, and let them marinate in the refrigerator for 4 hours (overnight is better). Turn the bags every hour or so.

Remove quail from the bags, drain and place on an oiled grill over hot coals, skin sides down, for 4-6 minutes or until the skin is browned and begins to crisp. Turn, and grill for 2 minutes or until the breast meat is cooked through.

Reheat some of the refrigerated sauce and spoon onto each serving plate, topping each with 2 quail.

Serves: 4

Mike Vail
NAHC Staff

Sweet Roasted Rabbit

- 2 rabbits, cleaned
- 1 cup orange juice
- 1 tsp. cayenne pepper
- 1 tsp. black pepper
- 1 T. sea salt
- 1½ tsp. ground fennel
- ⅛ tsp. nutmeg
- 2 T. lemon juice.
- ⅓ cup honey

Rinse the rabbits thoroughly and pat dry. On each rabbit, remove all four legs at the joint, but leave the loin in one piece. Place rabbit pieces in a large glass dish.

To make the marinade, heat the orange juice over medium heat until reduced by half, stirring occasionally. Remove from heat and let stand ten minutes. Then add the cayenne, black pepper, sea salt, fennel, nutmeg and lemon juice, stirring completely. Let stand another 10 minutes to let the flavors blend.

Add the honey to the orange juice mixture, stir and pour over the rabbit pieces, turning them to be sure they're all coated. Cover bowl and let sit at room temperature for 1½ hours, turning the pieces every 20 minutes.

Remove rabbit from marinade, drain and place on a rack in a roasting pan or on a cooking sheet. Roast in a 400 degree oven for 20-25 minutes or until done. Baste after ten minutes with the marinade and baste again right after removing from oven. Great with fresh-baked bread and honey butter.

Serves: 6-8

Mike Vail
NAHC Staff

Hoppin' John

- ½ lb. salt pork, diced
- 2 medium onions, coarsely chopped
- 2 cloves garlic, minced
- 3-4 celery stalks, chopped
- 2 10-oz. pkgs. frozen black eyed peas
- 4 cups water
- 2 tsp. salt
- ½ tsp. Tabasco (or to taste)
- 2 cups rice

In a large pot, fry salt pork over low heat until most of the fat has been rendered. Add onions, garlic and celery and cook over moderate heat until vegetables are soft, not brown. Add black eyed peas, water, salt and Tabasco. Bring to a boil, cover, reduce heat and simmer for 30 minutes. Stir in rice and cook until rice is tender and liquid is absorbed. Check seasoning, add salt and Tabasco to taste.

Serves: Serves a crowd!

Greg Carey
NAHC Staff

Venison

Easy Venison Steaks

4 venison steaks
2 medium onions, sliced
1 T. butter
   garlic, salt and pepper to taste

Heat shallow pan over medium heat. Season one side of venison with garlic, salt and pepper. When pan is hot, place butter in pan and melt. Put onions in pan and cook until onion sections separate. Place venison on top of onions, seasoned side down. Season top of venison with more garlic, salt and pepper. Cook on each side for 5-10 minutes (5 minutes for rare, 10 minutes for well-done). Serve immediately.

Serves: 4

Michael Forbes
Brighton, Michigan

Fried Venison Liver

1 deer liver, thinly sliced
1 cup flour, seasoned with salt and pepper
2 large onions, sliced
   cooking oil

Place the seasoned flour on a large piece of waxed paper. Heat ⅓ cup cooking oil in a large frying pan over medium high heat. Add the onions and fry for about 5 minutes. Push the onions to one edge of the pan.

Coat each piece of liver with the seasoned flour. Place in pan and cook 2 minutes on each side. Don't overcook or the liver will be tough. As each batch is cooked, transfer to a pre-heated platter and keep warm in oven. When all of the liver is cooked, serve with onions on heated plates.

A chilled liver will be easier to slice. If possible, place liver in freezer for an hour before slicing. Use a sharp knife to cut the slices as thinly as possible.

Serves: 6-12, depending on liver size

Carl Dudley
Newport, Oregon

Italian Venison

3 lb. venison roast
2½ cups water
1 large onion, chopped
½ tsp. salt
½ tsp. onion salt
½ tsp. garlic salt
½ tsp. oregano

¼ tsp. basil
½ tsp. Italian seasoning
½ tsp. seasoned salt
1 tsp. Accent
1 tsp. black pepper
   pepperoncinis

Place venison in roaster pan and add water. Add onion and salt. Cover and bake at 300 degrees until roast crumbles apart. There will be quite a bit of broth. Let meat set in broth in refrigerator overnight. Next day, tear up meat and with broth, add remaining ingredients to roasting pan. Cook on top of stove or in low oven for 2-3 hours. Meat will absorb most of the broth as it cooks. Add a little beef broth if necessary. The longer this cooks, the more the flavors will blend.

During the last 30 minutes of cooking, add several pepperoncinis, depending on your taste. Serve with pepperoncinis, if desired.

Serves: 6-8

Clara Sawlaw
Paris, Illinois

Venison Bologna

4 lbs. ground venison
¼ cup quick salt
1 tsp. garlic powder
2 T. mustard seed

2 tsp. black pepper
3 tsp. sugar
4 tsp. liquid smoke seasoning

Mix all ingredients, except liquid smoke, in large bowl and refrigerate overnight. Next day, add liquid smoke seasoning and mix well again. Shape in approximately 1 pound rolls (logs). Bake on a cookie sheet for 1¼ hours at 300 degrees. To make garlic bologna, double garlic powder. To make hot bologna, add 3 tablespoons hot pepper seed or 1 tablespoon cayenne pepper.

Serves: Many

Alton Summers
Alexandria, Virginia

31

Jess's Deer Chili

1½ lbs. ground venison
½ onion, chopped
1 T. chili pepper
1 tsp. hot red pepper
1 28-oz. can tomatoes
1 16-oz. can kidney beans
¾ cup barbecue sauce
    cooking oil (as needed)

In large pot, brown meat in 2 tablespoons oil and drain. Remove meat from pot. Heat 1 tablespoon oil in pot, add onions and cook until tender. Add meat and remaining ingredients. Bring to a boil, then decrease heat and simmer for 20 minutes, stirring occasionally.

Serves: 6-8

Jess Gilland
Onida, South Dakota

Quick Ground Venison Stroganoff

1 lb. ground venison
1 can cream of mushroom soup
1 cup milk
8 oz. sour cream
½ cup onion, chopped (optional)
1 cup fresh mushrooms, sliced (optional)

Brown meat, add salt and pepper to taste. Add onion, mushrooms, soup and milk. Mix together and simmer for 15 minutes. Add sour cream and simmer only 3 more minutes. Serve over white rice or noodles.

Serves: 4

Leslie Horton
Hillsboro, Missouri

Venison Goulash

2 lbs. venison, cubed
¼ cup oil
1 large onion, chopped
2 large garlic cloves, chopped
¼ cup flour
1 T. Hungarian paprika

1 13-oz. can beef broth
1½ cups water
1 8-oz. can tomato sauce
1 bay leaf
salt and pepper to taste

Heat oil in Dutch oven. Add onions and garlic and saute until onions are translucent. Remove onions and garlic and set aside. Toss venison cubes in flour and shake off excess. Brown venison in Dutch oven. Add paprika to venison. Saute about 1 minute, stirring constantly. Return onion and garlic to pan. Add remaining ingredients and simmer until tender, about 1 hour. Serve with buttered noodles.

Serves: 4-6

Fredrick H. Vobis
Phillipsport, New York

Spicy Venison Jerky

3-4 lbs. venison, sliced, 1" wide and ¼" thick
¼ cup soy sauce
1¼ cup Worcestershire sauce
1 T. liquid smoke seasoning
1 T. quick salt
2 tsp. hot sauce
½ tsp. cayenne pepper
½ tsp. garlic powder
¼ cup brown sugar
1 T. black pepper

Mix all ingredients completely except venison. Add meat and let stand in refrigerator for 12-24 hours, stirring 3 or 4 times. Drain meat on paper towels and spread on racks of dehydrator. Heat until dry but not brittle. Store in refrigerator.

Yields: 24-36 jerky strips

Lonnie Smith
Petersburg, Pennsylvania

Onion Mushroom
Venison Roast

3-4 lb. venison roast
1 large onion, quartered
2-3 potatoes, quartered
1 pkg. dried onion soup mix
1 can cream of mushroom soup
¾ cup water
2-3 carrots, peeled and cut into chunks

Line roasting pan with aluminum foil for easier clean-up.

Spread onion soup mix in bottom of pan. Place roast on onion soup mix. Top meat with cream of mushroom soup. Place vegetables around meat. Pour water around meat. Cover and cook at 325 degrees for 3 hours.

Optional: Can be done in a slow cooker prior to going out for the morning hunt and will be ready for evening supper.

Serves: 8

John Butler
Bear, Delaware

Venison Steak with Onion

3 lbs. venison steaks
2 onions, sliced
1 cup tomato soup
1 T. vinegar
1 T. Worcestershire sauce

2 T. brown sugar
½ cup water
salt to taste
oil for frying

Fry steaks in oil until cooked rare. Cover steaks with onions and simmer for 30 minutes. Mix remaining ingredients and pour over steak and onions. Bake at 325 degrees for 1 hour. Add more water as needed.

Serves: 6-8

Stephen Holmes
Charlottetown, Prince Edward Island

Delicious Venison Burgers

   2 lbs. ground venison
   ¼ lb. beef suet (fat)
   1 onion, chopped
   4 slices of fresh bread, torn into small pieces
   1 tsp. salt
   ¼ tsp. pepper

Mix the venison, fat, onion and bread. Add salt and pepper. Make into patties and fry or broil as for hamburgers.

Serves: 4-6

Stephen Holmes
Charlottetown, Prince Edward Island

Venison Meat Pie

   2 lbs. pork and 2 lbs. venison, ground together
   4 medium onions, chopped
   2 T. cooking oil
  12 potatoes, cooked and mashed with milk and butter
   1 tsp. allspice
   ½ tsp. cinnamon
   4 ready made pie crusts
     salt and pepper to taste

Cook onions and meat in oil until done.

In large pan, mix mashed potatoes, cooked meat, onions and spices. Fill pie crust with this mixture and add top crust. Bake at 350 degrees until crust is nicely browned.

For freezing, bake only ½ hour and when ready to eat, butter top and bake until lightly browned and heated completely.

Yields: 2 pies

Michael A. Bue
Lowell, Massachusetts

Venison Liver and Onions

1 liver, sliced ½" thick
¼ cup lemon juice
1 cup flour
1 tsp. salt

½ tsp. pepper
8 slices bacon
4 large onions, sliced

Rinse liver in cold salted water and blot dry with paper towels. Soak in lemon juice for 30 minutes, turning frequently, and drain. Combine flour, salt and pepper in resealable plastic bag. Add liver and shake.

Fry bacon until done. Remove and keep warm. Fry onions in bacon drippings until golden, remove and keep warm. Slowly fry liver in bacon fat 15-20 minutes. Cover with bacon and onions and simmer for 10 minutes.

Serves: 4-6

Stephen Holmes
Charlottetown, Prince Edward Island

Venison Marsala

1½ lbs. venison round steak
    garlic, salt and pepper to taste
    flour

1 T. butter
1 cup sliced mushrooms
3 oz. dry marsala wine

Season venison with garlic, salt and pepper or use your favorite spices. Sprinkle light coating of flour evenly over meat. Pound flour and spices into both sides of meat - the edge of a thin saucer works well, making a crisscross pattern to tenderize.

Heat butter in skillet on high heat until butter starts to scorch. Place meat in pan, leaving on high heat until golden brown. Turn and repeat on other side until done. Remove from pan and set aside.

Reduce heat, add mushrooms to pan and saute lightly and quickly. Add wine and stir for 1 minute over high heat. Pour mushrooms, wine and contents of pan over steak. Other vegetables can be sauteed with mushrooms if desired.

Serves: 4

Richard Kaehr
Fort Wayne, Indiana

Don's Venison Jerky

4 lbs. venison	1 cup soy sauce
½ tsp. salt	1 cup Worcestershire
¼ tsp. red pepper	sauce
1 tsp. lemon pepper	¼ tsp. garlic powder
1 tsp. black pepper	1 tsp. onion salt
¼ tsp. liquid smoke seasoning	4 T. ketchup

Slice meat ¼" thick or thinner. Mix remaining ingredients together well. Put meat in liquid in a covered dish and refrigerate at least 12 hours, longer is better. Take out and pat on a paper towel to get excess liquid off and put in dehydrator for 6 hours or until dry and rubbery.

Yields: 36-48 jerky strips

Donald Ralston
Springdale, Arizona

Venison Stew

½ lb. venison, cut in small pieces	2-3 celery stalks, sliced
1 can beef stock	1 small onion, chopped
1 large can whole tomatoes	3-4 carrots, sliced
2 large cans tomato sauce	2-3 potatoes, cut in small pieces
1 T. garlic powder	
½ tsp. Greek seasoning	
½ tsp. Cajun spice	
1 tsp. seasoning salt	

Pressure cook venison for about 30 minutes or according to your pressure cooker's instructions. Take meat off bones, rinse with water and cut into small pieces.

Mix beef stock, tomatoes and tomato sauce in slow cooker. Add meat and spices. Add celery, onion and carrots and cook until carrots begin to get tender. Add potatoes and cook until done. Check flavor and add more spices to suit your taste.

Serves: 4

Donald Ralston
Springdale, Arizona

Kevin's Easy Venison Jerky

2 lb. venison roast
2 tsp. liquid smoke
2 tsp. salt
2 tsp. garlic powder
2 tsp. Accent
2 tsp. onion powder
2 tsp. black pepper
½ cup Worcestershire
   sauce
½ cup soy sauce

Kevin M. Magee

Slice venison about ⅛" thick and set aside. Mix all other ingredients in a large bowl and stir together well. Add venison meat and toss with seasonings. Marinate overnight.

Lay meat in a single layer on food dehydrator racks for up to 16 hours until dry and chewy. Rotate racks after 8 hours (rotate top rack to the bottom and bottom to the top).

If you don't have a food dehydrator, you can nake jerky in the oven. Preheat to lowest setting, not much higher than 120 degrees. Arrange meat on racks and cook in oven for 4-6 hours or until leathery but still flexible. Monitor oven temperature frequently and if it exceeds 120 degrees, prop door open with a ball of aluminum foil or an empty can.

Yields: 24-36 jerky strips

Kevin M. Magee
Prescott, Wisconsin

Marinated Roast Venison

3-4 lbs. venison roast
  1 cup red wine
  1 pkg. dried onion soup mix
  1 can cream of mushroom soup

Marinate meat in wine overnight. Remove meat and place on a large sheet of foil. Mix mushroom soup and onion soup mix with wine. Pour over meat and seal foil well. Cook at 325 degrees for 2½ hours or until tender.

Serves: 6-8

Richard Weber
Martin, Tennessee

Mexican Venison Casserole

1½ lbs. ground venison
  1 small onion, chopped
  1 can cream of mushroom soup
  1 can mild enchilada sauce
  1 can mushrooms

1 can evaporated milk
2 cups cheddar cheese, shredded
  salt and pepper to taste
  white corn tortilla chips

Brown meat along with onion until well done (it will be coarsely crumbled). Add all remaining ingredients except corn chips and cheese. Cook over low heat for 15 minutes. Crush tortilla chips and put a 1-2" layer in the bottom of a 9" x 13" pan. Pour meat mixture over top of chips and mix together lightly. Top with cheese. Bake at 350 degrees for 30-45 minutes until bubbly and lightly browned. Let set 10 minutes, then serve.

You can top this off with chopped onion, tomatoes, lettuce, olives, guacamole or any favorite Mexican toppings. Great as a main dish or as a side dish with corn chips for dipping.

Serves: 6-8

Rosie Conroy
Traverse City, Michigan

Spicy Venison Sausage

4-5 lbs. venison
1½ lbs. salted pork
¼ tsp. ground allspice
¼ tsp. ground nutmeg
¼ tsp. ground cloves
½ tsp. black pepper
1½ tsp. garlic

1-2 tsp. crushed red peppers
1-2 tsp. ground cayenne pepper
2 T. fennel seed

Trim all excess fat and scrap from venison. Grind venison and salted pork. Mix together and regrind. Mix remaining ingredients in a small bowl. Add spices to meat mixture and mix well. Divide into appropriate portions and freeze. This sausage is great for breakfast or spaghetti sauce.

Yields: 6-8 sausage patties per pound

Michael Madden
Troy, New York

Barbecued Venison Ribs

6 lbs. venison ribs
3 tsp. venison seasoning
1½ cups ketchup
⅓ cup brown sugar
1 T. molasses
1 T. Worcestershire sauce
1 T. prepared mustard

¼ tsp. chili powder
1 large onion, diced

Season ribs with venison seasoning and let stand 30 minutes. Mix remaining ingredients well to make a sauce. Dip ribs into the sauce and place in a roaster or baking dish. Pour the remaining sauce over the top. Bake, uncovered, 3-4 hours at 300 degrees until tender and brown, turning once or twice to coat with sauce.

Serves: 8

Doug Wohlwend
Muskego, Wisconsin

Rocky Mountain Crockpot Roast

3-4 lbs. venison
  1 8-oz. can tomato sauce
  3 T. Worcestershire sauce
  2 T. soy sauce
  5 carrots sticks, chopped
  5 medium sized potatoes, diced
  1 medium yellow onion, diced
  1 cup celery, chopped

1½ cups water
  seasoned salt to taste
  dash of Tabasco sauce
  dash of chili powder
  pepper to taste
2 T. flour
1 T. water

Combine all ingredients in a standard Crockpot and cook 8-10 hours on low or 5 hours on high. Separate the carrots and potatoes from the venison after cooking. Remove the meat from the Crockpot and make gravy of the remains in the Crockpot which can be thickened by adding a mixture of flour and water.

Serves: 6-8

Wayne F. LeDoux
Colorado Springs, Colorado

Stewed Venison Meatloaf

2 lbs. ground venison
1 tsp. dry mustard
1 16-oz. can stewed tomatoes
½ tsp. black pepper
¼ tsp. garlic powder
1 lb. bacon, fried and crumbled
1 cup bread crumbs

1 cup bell pepper, chopped
1 large onion, chopped
2 eggs, beaten

Preheat oven to 300 degrees. Mix all ingredients. Shape into a loaf and place in a large baking dish. Cover with foil and bake for 2 hours, checking after ½ hour. Drain off any accumulated fat and continue baking until 2 hours are up.

Serves: 4-6

Dick Baker
Lima, Ohio

Dick's Venison Roast

    2 bs. venison roast
       Lawry's seasoned salt
       parsley flakes
       Prudhomme's Meat Magic
       pepper
    1 can cream of mushroom soup
    ½ cup milk

Sprinkle roast liberally with seasoned salt, parsley flakes, Meat Magic and pepper. Place roast in roasting pan. Mix together soup and milk and pour around roast (do not wash off seasoning). Cook on medium heat 3-4 hours.

Goes great with boiled potatoes and corn. You can also add potatoes to pot 1 hour before roast is done.

Serves: 4

Dick Baker
Lima, Ohio

Kenny's Microwave Meatloaf

    2 lbs. ground venison
    2 slices bread, crumbled
    ½ cup cracker crumbs
    1 pkg. dried onion soup mix
    ¼ cup milk
    2 eggs, beaten
    1 T. Worcestershire sauce

    ½ cup onions, minced (optional)
    2 oz. mushrooms, sliced (optional)
    ½ T. garlic salt (optional)
    ½ cup ketchup
    1 T. mustard
    3 T. brown sugar

Mix first 10 ingredients and place in a 12" x 8" x 2" microwave dish. Then mix ketchup, mustard and brown sugar and pour on top of meatloaf. Cover and place in microwave, cook on high for 18-20 minutes or until done, turning dish 90 degrees every 5 minutes. Cooking time will vary depending on power of your microwave.

Serves: 6-8

Kenneth Crummett
Sugar Grove, West Virginia

Mike's Bold Venison Jerky

3 lbs. venison roast
1 cup A-1 Bold Steak Sauce
1 cup soy sauce
1 cup Worcestershire sauce
½ cup barbecue sauce

2 tsp. Accent
2 tsp. seasoned salt
2 tsp. onion powder
2 tsp. black pepper
1 tsp. garlic powder

Slice venison ¼" thick by 2" wide. Remove all excess fat. Layer in oblong container with sealed lid. After every other layer, cover with some of the marinade sauce. Seal container tight and refrigerate for 12 hours. Flip container over and refrigerate for another 12 hours.

Place strips in a dehydrator and cook for 48 hours. Rotate racks after 24 hours.

Yields: 36-48 jerky strips

Michael Narlock
Watertown, Wisconsin

Ozark Venison Roast

4 lbs. venison roast
2 cloves garlic, minced
1 large onion, sliced
2 T. brown sugar

1 tsp. prepared mustard
1 T. Worcestershire sauce
¼ cup vinegar or lemon juice
1 14-oz. can tomatoes, chopped

Marinade:

½ c. vinegar
2 T. salt
2 cloves garlic, minced
1-2 cups cold water

Mix marinade ingredients together and add roast. Allow venison to stand overnight in marinade in the refrigerator. Drain and place meat and remaining ingredients in Crockpot. Cook for 8-10 hours.

Serves: 8

Kevin Burbridge
Shell Knob, Missouri

Mule Deer Stroganoff

     2 lbs. mule deer steak
     ⅛ cup butter
     1 cup chopped onion
     ¼ tsp. dried minced garlic
     ½ tsp. paprika
     ½ tsp. black pepper
     2 cans cream of mushroom soup
     ½ cup water
     1 cup sour cream

Slice steak into 1" cubes. Saute in butter until lightly browned. Stir in onion, garlic, paprika and pepper. In a bowl, combine soup and water, stir until smooth, and add to meat. Cover and simmer until meat is tender, stirring occasionally. Stir in sour cream. Cook an additional 5-10 minutes, but do not boil. Serve over cooked noodles, rice or baked potatoes.

Serves: 6

Jody Stampe
Gillette, Wyoming

Tasty Venison Bologna

     5 lbs. ground venison
     5 tsp. salt
  1½ tsp. salt
     3 tsp. mustard seed
     3 tsp. coarse black pepper
     3 tsp. garlic salt

Mix all ingredients well and separate into 2 or 3 parts. Roll each part into a log, cover with plastic wrap and place in refrigerator for 3 days. Place rolls on a wire rack in a 9" x 13" baking pan. Bake in oven for 1 hour at 350 degrees.

Yields: 3 rolls of bologna

Leonard Kozlosky
Shenandoah, Pennsylvania

Wild Indian Stew

2 lbs. venison stew meat
1 large can tomato sauce
1 cup water
2 T. oil
4 green peppers, chopped
6 carrots, thickly sliced
1 head cauliflower
   (broken into florets)

2 onions, chopped
¼ tsp. garlic powder
2 large potatoes, cubed
2 bay leaves
1 large can tomato sauce
   dash of thyme, rosemary and basil
   salt and pepper to taste

Put venison in a sauce pan, sprinkle with garlic powder and fry until browned. Cover with tomato sauce and water, stir and simmer for about 1 hour. Add the vegetables, except the cauliflower, which is to be added 15 minutes before serving time. Add additional water as necessary. This stew is excellent, it's even better if cooked the day before serving, refrigerated and then heated for the next day's meal.

Serves: 8

Gerald Davis
Dumont, New Jersey

Venison and Gravy

2-3 venison steaks, cut into pieces
  2 onions, sliced
  1 can cream of mushroom soup
  1 can cream of onion soup

Fry steak and onions until steak is cooked rare. Pour steak and onions into baking dish (for flavor, include the drippings from pan). Mix soups together and pour over venison and onions in baking dish. Bake at 400 degrees until gravy thickens to your taste.

Serves: 4

Marc and Melinda Morris
Roanoke, Virginia

Venison Tamale Pie

- 1 lb. ground venison
- 1 12-oz. can corn or mexicorn
- 1 8-oz. can tomato sauce
- 1 1½ oz. pkg. taco seasoning mix
- 1 can refrigerator buttermilk biscuits, 7½ oz. or larger
- 4 oz. cheddar cheese, shredded

Preheat oven to 350 degrees. Brown venison and drain. Add corn, tomato sauce and taco seasoning. Stir well and set aside. Separate biscuits and arrange in a greased pie pan. Press biscuits together over bottom and up sides of pan to form a crust. Spoon venison mixture into crust. Bake for 20 minutes. Sprinkle with cheddar cheese and return to oven for an additional 5 minutes until crust is golden brown and cheese melts. Let stand 5 minutes before cutting.

Serves: 6-8

Karen Witman
N. Irwin, Pennsylvania

Madison Stroganoff

- 1 lb. ground venison
- ½ cup diced onion
- ½ tsp. garlic powder
- 1 4-oz. can sliced mushrooms
- 1 can cream of mushroom soup
- ¼ cup cheddar cheese, shredded
- ¼ cup pimento, chopped
- 2 T. flour
- ¼ tsp. pepper
- 1 cup sour cream

Brown venison, breaking into small chunks. Add all remaining ingredients, except sour cream. Cover and cook on low heat 20 minutes, stirring once or twice. Stir in sour cream, mix thoroughly and heat but do not boil. Pour in a serving dish and sprinkle with parsley, if desired. Serve over cooked rice or noodles.

Serves: 4

Laurie Lunenschloss
Madison, Wisconsin

Barbecued Meatballs

1 lb. ground venison
1 T. Worcestershire sauce
1 T. vinegar
2 T. sugar
½ cup ketchup
½ cup beer

Roll ground venison into 1" balls.

Mix remaining ingredients in sauce pan and simmer briskly for 15 minutes. Remove from heat and set aside. Broil meatballs, turning to brown on all sides. Drain, add to sauce and simmer for 30-45 minutes.

These meatballs are better if made ahead and they freeze well.

Yields: 30 small meatballs

Laurie Klunenschloss
Madison, Wisconsin

Madison Deer Loaf

1½ lbs. ground venison
½ lb. mild Italian sausage
1 lb. hamburger
½ cup finely diced onions
    basil, garlic, salt and pepper to taste

Mix all ingredients together and bake in loaf pan at 350 degrees for 1½ to 2 hours.

Serves: 4-6

Laurie Klunenschloss
Madison, Wisconsin

Montana Surprise

2 lbs. deer burger

1 lb. bulk pork sausage
   (your favorite flavor)

1½ cups elbow macaroni or
   egg noodles

1 12-oz. jar of beef, chicken
   or turkey gravy

1 green pepper, chopped

1 yellow onion, diced

½ head cabbage, chopped in
   large pieces

1 T. chopped garlic

1 T. chopped jalapeno pepper
   (optional)

salt and pepper to taste

In a large bowl, mix the deer burger with the sausage, then brown the mixture in frying pan, making sure that the mix is broken up.

Boil the elbow macaroni or noodles and set aside.

Put the deer/pork mix in a large pot and mix with the gravy, green pepper, onion and cabbage. Add the garlic, salt, black pepper, jalapeno pepper and any other spices you like. Simmer for about 1 hour or until it is done to your liking. Add the macaroni or noodles for the last 15 minutes.

Serves: 8

Frank E. Kosloski
Oceanside, California

Frank E. Kosloski

Swedish Meatballs

1 lb. ground venison
¼ lb. mild pork sausage
1 egg, slightly beaten
1 cup milk
  enough coarse bread to be absorbed in milk
1 tsp. salt
½ tsp. pepper
1 T. Accent
¼ tsp. nutmeg
1 small onion, chopped

Mix all ingredients thoroughly, should be rather moist. Add more milk if necessary. Roll into small balls and fry, turning constantly. Do not overcook.

Yields: 24 meatballs

Laurie Klunenschloss
Madison, Wisconsin

Jill's Crumby Venison

10 venison cutlets, ¼" thick
  salt and pepper to taste
1 pint sour cream
½ bag seasoned stuffing mix
2 T. butter

Place cutlets on a baking sheet and season with salt and pepper. Cover the cutlets with sour cream, about ¼ - ½" thick. Sprinkle the dry stuffing mix over the sour cream. Put thin strips of butter over the stuffing to prevent it from burning.

Bake in oven at 350 degrees for ½ hour or until stuffing is browned.

Serves: 4

Clifton Cornelison
Flanders, New Jersey

Venison Pasta Salad

8 cups cooked venison, cut into bitesized cubes
1 lb. red, white and green spiral pasta (cooked al dente and drained)
1 large can pitted black olives, drained and sliced
1 large sweet onion, chopped
1 red bell pepper, chopped
1 green pepper, chopped
4 cloves fresh garlic, minced
1 16-oz. bottle Italian dressing

Toss all ingredients together. Chill 3-6 hours, tossing occasionally. Serve chilled.

Serves: 12 (as a side dish)

Bob Blazer
Waterford Works, New Jersey

Venison Pepper Steak with Rice

1-2 lbs. venison, cut into
    thin slices
1-2 T. cooking oil
2 large onions, sliced
2-3 large peppers, sliced
    (green, red or yellow)
1 T. Worcestershire sauce
1 T. soy sauce

1-2 cups water
2 T. flour mixed with 2 T. water
salt and pepper to taste
rice, cooked

Pour oil in electric skillet and heat briefly. Add onions and peppers and let cook until tender (5-10 minutes on 350 degrees). With a slotted spoon, remove onions and peppers from skillet. Put meat in skillet, add Worcestershire sauce and soy sauce. Brown meat well. When meat is brown, add peppers, onions, salt and pepper, together with 1-2 cups water. Let all ingredients simmer about 25-30 minutes. Mix flour and water to make a paste and add to meat and vegetables, stirring until sauce thickens. Simmer for an additional 10 minutes. Serve over rice.

Serves: 4-6

William E. Hicks
Gloucester County, Virginia

Foiled Onion Steak

2 venison round steaks
1 pkg. dried onion soup mix

Tear 2 sheets of foil big enough to enclose each steak. Sprinkle one-fourth of the onion soup mix over the middle of each sheet of foil. Lay a steak on top of soup mix. Sprinkle the remaining soup mix over the steaks. Fold the foil around each steak and seal. Place on a cookie sheet and bake at 350 degrees about 45 minutes.

Serves: 2

Arland Yesse
Berlin, Wisconsin

Venison Swiss Steak in Sour Cream Gravy

1½ lbs. venison steak
¼ cup flour
1 T. dry mustard
1 tsp. salt
1 tsp. dried thyme leaves
¼ tsp. pepper
1 T. vegetable oil

1 16-oz. can stewed tomatoes
1 large onion, sliced
½ cup celery, diced
2 large carrots, diced
1 T. brown sugar
½ cup sour cream

Cut meat into serving sized pieces and spread on waxed paper. Mix flour, mustard, salt, thyme and pepper; sprinkle over all sides of meat. Cover with another piece of waxed paper. Pound meat, using a mallet, until flour and spice mixture is worked into meat.

Heat oil in a heavy casserole or Dutch oven and brown meat. Add tomatoes, onion, celery, carrots and brown sugar. Cover and simmer for 1½ hours or until tender. Just before serving, stir sour cream into gravy.

This dish is best when cooked slowly and makes its own gravy.

Serves: 4

Arland Yesse
Berlin, Wisconsin

Joe's Fried Venison

2 lbs. venison steak
1½ tsp. salt
½ tsp. black pepper
1 T. liquid smoke seasoning
1 package meat marinade
1 cup water

¼ cup flour
2 T. bacon grease
¾ cup chopped celery
2 small onions, sliced
1 T. Worcestershire sauce
2 cups canned whole tomatoes

Cut venison into serving size pieces. Mix salt, pepper, liquid smoke seasoning and marinade mix in water. Place in plastic container with lid and shake. Add venison and let stand 30-60 minutes. Drain meat on paper towels. Dip venison in flour and brown on all sides in a large skillet in the bacon grease. Add celery, onions and Worcestershire sauce. Cook until tender. Add undrained tomatoes and let simmer for 1½ - 2 hours, or longer on older venison.

Serves: 6

Joseph Mercer
Ashland, Ohio

Venison Pot Pie

double pie crust for 9" pie
2 cups cooked venison
⅓ cup butter
⅓ cup flour
1 T. onion flakes
1 T. beef soup base

½ tsp. salt
¼ tsp. pepper
1¾ cup water
⅔ cup milk
1 10-oz. pkg. frozen peas and carrots

In large pot, heat butter until melted. Stir in flour, onion flakes, soup base, salt and pepper. Add water and milk, stirring constantly. Heat to boiling and boil 1 minute while stirring. Stir in venison, peas and carrots. Pour into pie crust and top with second pie crust. Bake at 425 degrees for 30-35 minutes, until brown. Let stand 15 minutes before serving.

Serves: 6-8

Jesse Sias
Glendale, Arizona

Venison Barbecue Beans

1 lb. venison. cubed in small pieces
1 20-oz. can pork and beans
½ cup barbecue sauce
1-2 tsp. chili powder
1 tsp. brown sugar
¼ tsp. salt

Brown venison in heavy skillet. Add pork and beans, barbecue sauce, chili powder, brown sugar and salt. Cook 20 minutes until meat is tender and flavors well blended.

Serves: 8-12

Dan Bartlett
Northfield, New Hampshire

Texas Venison Kabobs

1 16-oz. aged venison (preferably backstrap)
1 lb. lean sliced bacon
lemon pepper

Slice the venison across the grain about ¾" thick. Slice and trim fat from meat. Cut the meat into ¾" strips, and again into ¾" cubes.

Take a strip of bacon and push the very end of the bacon on the skewer. Next push a venison cube on the skewer and fold the bacon over and push the skewer through the bacon. Repeat until the bacon slice has been used up. The bacon will appear to be woven back and forth around the venison cubes.

One slice of bacon will weave around 7-8 venison cubes per skewer, depending on the length. You may also experiment by adding vegetables such as cherry tomatoes, onions, peppers, mushrooms or squash.

Sprinkle the kabobs with lemon pepper and refrigerate overnight. Cook over a hot bed of coals. The bacon will prevent the venison from drying out.

Serves: 8

Dr. Lloyd J. Taylor, III, P.E.
Wichita Falls, Texas

Venison Burgers Deluxe

2 T. butter
1½ cups fresh mushrooms, sliced
½ cup clear beef broth

½ tsp. tarragon
1 14-oz. can chopped tomatoes and juice

Melt butter in skillet and saute mushrooms for 3-4 minutes. Add broth, tarragon and chopped tomatoes with juice and simmer.

2 T. butter
2 tsp. teriyaki sauce
1 lb. ground venison

In another skillet, melt butter and add teriyaki sauce. Fry venison burgers to desired doneness, approximately 5-7 minutes per side for medium. Pour tomato mixture over burgers for a quick and easy entree.

Serves: 4

Leonard Simmons
Waterville, New York

Venison in Sour Cream

2 lbs. venison, stew meat cut
    in 1" cubes
4 slices bacon, diced
1 small onion, chopped
1 garlic clove, minced
2 tsp. salt

¼ tsp. pepper
½ tsp. crumbled, dried marjoram
⅔ cup dry white wine
2 cups sour cream

Cook bacon in kettle until browned, remove and set aside. Add venison to fat remaining in kettle and brown on all sides. Add onions and garlic and cook for a few minutes. Stir in bacon and onion, clove, salt and pepper. Bring to a boil, cover and simmer for 1½ hours, or until meat is tender. Add a little broth or water if mixture becomes dry. Stir in sour cream and heat gently but do not boil.

Serves: 4-6

Galen Vesnefsky
Medford, Wisconsin

Cranberry Venison Meatballs

Meatballs

2 lbs. ground venison	1 T. parsley flakes
2 eggs, beaten	2 T. dehydrated onion
1 cup cornflake crumbs	½ tsp. salt
⅓ cup ketchup	¼ tsp. pepper
2 T. soy sauce	

Sauce

1 16-oz. can jellied cranberry sauce	3 T. brown sugar
1 cup ketchup	1 T. lemon juice

Combine meatball ingredients in a mixing bowl and mix well. Shape into 72 meatballs (1" each). Place in a 15" x 10" x 1" baking pan. Bake at 350 degrees for 20-25 minutes or until done. Remove from the oven and drain on paper towels.

In a large pot, combine sauce ingredients. Cook, stirring frequently, until the cranberry sauce is melted. Add the meatballs and heat thoroughly.

Yields: 72 meatballs

Galen Vesnefsky
Medford, Wisconsin

Dick's Venison Jerky

2 lbs. venison	¼ cup soy sauce
1 T. Worcestershire sauce	¼ tsp. pepper
¼ tsp. garlic powder	½ tsp. onion powder
1 tsp. salt	

Cut meat into strips 1" wide by ¼" - ½" thick. Remove all fat. Combine all ingredients. Place meat in marinade and cover tightly. Refrigerate at least 8 hours, stirring often. Dry meat on paper towels and cook on rack in oven set at lowest temperature, until firm (about 4-6 hours).

Yields: 18-24 jerky strips

Dick Baker
Lima, Ohio

West Virginia Venison Chili & Dumplings

4 lbs. venison, coarsely ground
3 T. cooking oil
2 cup chopped onions
1 green pepper, diced fine
1 celery stalk, diced fine
4 garlic cloves, diced fine
2 cans chili beans
2 bay leaves

1 28-oz. can tomatoes, crushed
1 8-oz. can tomato paste
2 cups venison stock or 1 can beef stock
4 T. chili powder
1 tsp. oregano
2 T. cayenne pepper or crushed red
   hot peppers

Heat oil in a 5 quart Dutch oven. Add onions, peppers, celery and garlic and saute until tender. Add venison and saute until brown. Add remaining ingredients and cook on medium heat for 1 hour, then reduce heat and simmer gently for an additional 1/2 hour. Remove bay leaves.

Dumplings

½ cup flour
¾ cup cornmeal
2 tsp. baking powder
½ tsp. salt
½ cup milk
1 T. cooking oil

Mix the dumpling ingredients together until combined and moistened. Drop dumplings into pot with a tablespoon. Cover to cook dumplings — DO NOT UNCOVER FOR AT LEAST 15 MINUTES or until you think the dumplings are done. Garnish with diced spanish onions (optional).

Serves: 8-12

Ralph L. Ansley, Jr.
Fort Ashby, West Virginia

Venison Steak in Mushroom Sauce

4 venison steaks, cut in serving pieces
   flour to coat steaks
½ stick butter or margarine
1 can cream of mushroom soup
10 oz. milk

Dust both sides of venison pieces with flour. Melt butter in a frying pan over medium-high heat, add meat and brown on both sides. While steak is browning, mix soup and milk together until well blended. Pour over browned meat and simmer for 20 minutes, stirring occasionally. Add more milk and reduce heat if the sauce becomes too thick.

Serves: 4

Duane Wolfgang
Williamstown, Pennsylvania

Don's Totally Awesome Venison Chili

2½ lbs. venison
   olive oil to brown meat
1 large onion, coarsely chopped
3 garlic cloves, minced
1 tsp. paprika
5 T. chili powder
2 tsp. ground cumin
1 tsp. dried oregano
⅓ tsp. cayenne pepper
1 14-oz. can diced tomatoes
1 15-oz. can tomato sauce
1 tsp. salt
1 12-oz. can dark beer
1 small green pepper, chopped
1 15-oz. can kidney beans

In a covered sauce pan or Dutch oven, heat the oil over medium high heat and cook the venison until it is evenly browned and no pink shows. Add onion and garlic and saute until the onion is translucent, about 5 minutes. Add the paprika, chili powder, cumin and oregano and stir 3 minutes to cook the spices. Add cayenne, tomatoes, tomato sauce, salt, beer and green pepper and stir to combine. Bring to a boil and simmer, covered, over low heat for 2 hours or until meat is tender, stirring occasionally and adding more beer as needed. Add beans and simmer for 30 minutes.

Serves: 15-20

Don Hoglund
Oberlin, Ohio

Venison & Asparagus
with Brandy Mushroom Sauce

1 cup Italian style bread crumbs
1 cup grated Parmesan/Romano cheese
1 tsp. coarse ground black pepper
2 eggs
   vegetable oil
1½ lbs. venison loin, cut into ¼" slices
2 lbs. asparagus
½ lb. mushrooms, cut into ¼" slices
1 T. butter
1 T. flour
¼ cup brandy
½ tsp. dry tarragon

½ tsp. dry mustard
¾ cup half and half
1 T. lemon juice

Mix bread crumbs, cheese and black pepper together. Beat eggs in a bowl. Dip meat pieces in egg and then roll in bread crumb mixture. Cover bottom of skillet with light coating of oil and heat. Brown meat (about 2-3 minutes per side). Set aside, keep warm.

Trim and discard tough end of asparagus, then rinse spears. Steam asparagus for about 10 minutes or until tender (if you don't have steamer, boil in about 2" of water). Saute mushrooms in butter over medium heat (about 3-4 minutes). Stir in flour and stir for about 1 minute.

In a separate small pan, warm brandy low heat until bubbly, then ignite (do not light under stove hood). Pour brandy into mushrooms when flames die down, stir and add tarragon, mustard and half and half. Stir until sauce is thickened. Remove from heat and stir in lemon juice.

Arrange venison and asparagus on plate and pour sauce over both.

Serves: 4

Dale Pinto
Bridgeville, Pennsylvania

Swiss Bliss Venison Steak

2 lbs. venison steak
½ tsp. butter, melted
1 package dried onion soup mix
½ lb. mushrooms, sliced (optional)
½ green pepper, sliced (optional)
1 lb. can tomatoes, drained and
    chopped (reserve juice) freshly
    ground pepper

¼ tsp. salt
1 T. cornstarch
1 T. A-1 Steak Sauce
2 T. chopped parsley

Line baking dish with foil. Spread butter over center of foil.

Cut steak into serving pieces. Arrange on foil, overlapping. Sprinkle with onion soup mix, mushrooms, green pepper, tomatoes, salt and pepper. Mix tomato juice, A-1 Steak Sauce and cornstarch. Pour over meat. Wrap venison with foil and double edges for a better seal.

Bake 2 hours at 375 degrees. Unwrap, place on serving platter and sprinkle with parsley.

Serves: 4

Duane Wolfgang
Williamstown, Pennsylvania

Venison Pot Roast

1 medium roast
16 oz. ketchup

1 12-oz. beer
1 package dried onion soup mix

Mix ketchup, beer and soup mix together. Line a roasting pan with two long sheets of foil. Pour half of sauce in bottom of pan. Place the roast on top and pour remaining sauce over the top. Seal foil pan air tight, so no steam can escape. Cook at 350 degrees for 3 hours. Serve with juices for dipping.

Serves: 8

Clair I. Kunz
Montpelier, Idaho

Pacific Northwest Venison

1½ lbs. venison steak, pounded thin
½ T. vegetable oil
2 garlic cloves, minced
1 small shallot, finely minced
10 oz. wild mushrooms
2 T. cornstarch
1½ cups chicken broth
salt and pepper to taste

Heat non-stick pan over medium high heat and add venison in batches, cooking quickly to medium rare, about 3 minutes, turning once. Remove meat from pan and cover with foil.

In same pan, add oil, garlic, shallot and mushrooms and saute, stirring frequently until ingredients are tender, about 3-4 minutes.

Dissolve cornstarch in broth. Increase heat to high and add broth to mushroom mixture along with any accumulated meat juices. Stir to thicken and heat through. Pour sauce over venison and serve.

Serves: 4

Diane Sandoval
Issaquah, Washington

Fajitas Texas Style

1½ lbs. venison
2 cans full bodied beer
1 tsp. salt
1 tsp. garlic
1 T. cooking oil
12 flour tortillas

Cut venison into ½" pieces, 3-4" long, and marinate in the beer, salt and garlic for approximately 2-3 hours. The best method is to put all ingredients in an extra large resealable plastic bag, seal and marinate. Shake the bag every 30 minutes to thoroughly mix all ingredients.

Drain meat. Coat non-stick skillet with cooking oil and cook venison until done. Serve on hot flour tortillas with your choice of garnishes. Squeeze lemon over all.

Garnish suggestions: lettuce, tomatoes, onion, sour cream, guacamole, salsa, black olives, sliced jalapeno peppers.

Serves: 4

Jack D. Hunter, II
Harlingen, Texas

Creole Venison Roast

2-3 lbs. venison roast
2-3 garlic cloves
2 medium onions, sliced thick
½ lb. fresh mushrooms, sliced thick
3 carrots, sliced into chunks

⅓ cup soy sauce
2 T. brown sugar
2 tsp. ginger
1 can tomato soup

Place roast in Dutch oven, stick garlic cloves into roast and cover with onion slices. Add mushrooms and carrots to Dutch oven. Mix remaining ingredients for sauce and pour over roast, mushrooms and carrots.

Cover and roast at 300 degrees for 4 hours. The roast makes its own gravy. Excellent when served with mashed potatoes or egg noodles. Can be cooked in a Crockpot (increase cooking time to 6-8 hours).

Serves: 8

Linda Hasselblad
Green Bay, Wisconsin

Venison Pozole

1½ lbs. venison meat, shredded
2 medium yellow onions, chopped
2 garlic cloves, crushed or 2 tsp. garlic powder
3 quarts water
1 T. salt - reduce for low or non-salt diets
4 medium to hot red chili pods
1 package pozole (white hominy), bulk or frozen (not canned)

In Crockpot, add all ingredients except for pozole and set Crockpot on high. Bring to a slow boil, approximately 1½ - 2 hours. Reduce heat to low. Cook for another 2 hours.

Add pozole and continue to cook for another hour. Let cool for about 3 hours. Skim off any fat from top of broth, remove chili pods and discard. Reheat, bringing broth to a slow simmer. Serve with tortillas, butter and crackers.

Serves: 8-10

Peter A. Goodman
Albuquerque, New Mexico

Wetzel's Venison Stew

1 medium (1-2 lb.) venison roast	4-5 potatoes, cut into bite sizes
seasoned salt	1 carrot, sliced
1 onion, sliced	1 can peas, drained
1 can cream of mushroom soup	1 stalk celery, sliced
	1 quart green beans

Place roast into a Crockpot and sprinkle with seasoned salt. Pour soup over roast and add onions. Cook until tender. Remove from pot, shred into pieces. Put back into pot, add vegetables and cook 2 hours. Make white sauce, add to stew and cook for an additional 1-2 hours.

White Sauce

2 T. butter	1 cup milk
2 T. flour	salt and pepper

Heat milk until warm. Blend melted butter and flour together and add to warm milk. Stir constantly until mixture thickens. Cook for 3 minutes longer, add salt and pepper and blend into stew.

Serves: 6-8

Wetzel Proffit
Warsaw, Ohio

Easy Venison Roast and Gravy

5-6 lb. venison roast	1 sprig fresh marjoram
¼ cup vegetable oil	1 clove garlic, minced
¼ tsp. salt	

Wipe roast with damp cloth and place in roaster. Combine ingredients and rub into roast. Cover and roast at 350 degrees for 25-30 minutes per pound, uncovering for the last half hour.

After roasting venison, remove from pan. Reserve juices and heat in Dutch oven until simmering. Add ½ cup sour cream and stir until gravy consistency.

Serves: 8-12

Stephen Holmes
Charlottetown, Prince Edward Island

Green Chili Elk Stew

1-2 lbs. shredded elk meat, preferably backstrap
2¼ cups pinto beans, bulk (not canned)
2½ quarts water
 10 medium to hot green chili pods, cayenne peppers
  1 large yellow onion
1-2 T. salt
  1 medium garlic clove, crushed or 2 tsp. garlic powder

VENISON

Wash pinto beans in cool water to get out all the dirt. Put beans into Crockpot with water and cook on low for 4-6 hours or until beans are pink in color, and unspotted. Add 1¼ quarts water to Crockpot.

While cooking beans, wash chili pods and cut off stems. Slice a small slit in pods and put onto cookie sheet. Broil chilis in oven until outer skin is black and peeling away from meat. Do not over roast! Turn pods until skin peels away from other side. Wash in cold water for 4 minutes, or until cool to touch. Peel off skin from pods and throw away skin. Clean out pods and then dice. Add chilis to Crockpot.

Add meat, onion, salt and garlic. Cook in Crockpot for 4-5 hours. Serve hot, with tortillas and sharp cheddar cheese. Add salt to taste.

Serves: 10-12

Peter A. Goodman
Albuquerque, New Mexico

Venison and Noodle Stew Mix

6 cups venison stew meat, diced
   and cooked
1 cup celery, sliced
1 up onion, sliced
1 cup carrots, sliced
¼ cup butter
½ tsp. marjoram

½ tsp. pepper
½ tsp. salt (optional)
1 T. parsley
1 bay leaf
8 beef bouillon cubes
4 oz. cooked noodles
9 cups water

Combine all ingredients in Crockpot and simmer for 1-2 hours.

Serves: 4-6

Dennis Wheeler
Marietta, Ohio

Slow Cooked Pepper Venison Steak

4 cups beef broth or venison stock
2 cups of your favorite noodles
2 lbs. venison steak
2 T. cooking oil
¼ cup soy sauce
½ cup chopped onion
2 garlic cloves, minced
1 tsp. sugar
½ tsp. salt
¼ tsp. pepper
¼ tsp. ground ginger
4 tomatoes, chopped or 1 16-oz. can tomatoes, chopped with liquid
2 large green or red peppers, cut into strips
½ cup cold water
1 T. cornstarch

Cook noodles in beef broth or stock and drain.

Cut venison into 3" x 1" strips. Brown in oil. Transfer to a slow cooker. Combine the next 7 ingredients and pour over venison. Cover and cook on low for 5-6 hours or until meat is tender. Add tomatoes and peppers and cook on low for 1 hour. Combine the cold water and cornstarch to make a paste. Stir into liquid in slow cooker and cook on high until thickened.

Serve over noodles.

Serves: 6-8

Jim Kaser
Millersburg, Ohio

Jiffy Teriyaki Steak

1 lb. venison rump steak
½ cup soy sauce
2 tsp. brown sugar
½ cup orange juice
1 tsp. fresh ginger, grated
1 clove, crushed

Cut meat into 1" cubes. Mix soy sauce, brown sugar, orange juice, ginger and garlic. Marinate the steak cubes in this mixture for 4-8 hours. Put meat on skewers and broil, basting frequently with the marinade, until done.

Serves: 4

Edna K. Hara
Los Angeles, California

Burger Bundles

1 lb. ground venison
⅓ cup evaporated milk or half-and-half
   chopped onion, as desired
1 cup seasoned stuffing mix

Sauce

1 can mushroom soup
2 T. Worcestershire sauce

1 T. ketchup

Combine venison, milk and onion and mix well. Divide meat into 4 pieces and pat out flat. Put ¼ cup stuffing mix on each and form nest around it with meat. Put in casserole.

Stir together sauce ingredients. Pour over meat. Bake at 350 degrees for 45-60 minutes.

Serves: 4

Becky Smith
Gibbon, Minnesota

Grilled Venison Marinade

2 lbs. venison steaks, ½-¾" thick
1 8-oz. bottled Italian dressing
1 can beer
½ cup water
1 package dried onion soup mix

2 T. Worcestershire sauce
1 T. Lawry's seasoned salt
1 tsp. garlic powder
1 tsp. fresh ground pepper

Combine all ingredients in baking pan and mix well. Place steaks in pan so they are completely covered by marinade. (If more marinade is needed to cover steaks, add more Italian dressing and beer.) Pierce each steak 3-4 times with a table fork so the marinade can be absorbed. Cover pan with foil and refrigerate for 4 hours. Drain steaks and grill for approximately 5 minutes per side over medium hot coals. Brush both sides of steaks with marinade after 5 minutes of grilling. This will help keep the steaks juicy.

Serves: 4

Kevin Schroeder
Aurora, Illinois

Joseph Smiljanich

Joe's All Purpose Marinade

    1 cup wine vinegar
    ½ cup soy sauce
 1½ tsp. salt
    ¼ tsp. pepper
    ¼ tsp. dried red pepper flakes
    ½ tsp. powder ginger
    1 T. dried minced onion
6-8 cloves garlic, crushed

Mix and stir vigorouly for 1-2 minutes. Immerse meat in the marinade for several hours or overnight, turning occasionally. Drain meat, then cook.

Serves: 24-36 pieces of jerky

Joseph Smiljanich
Wakefield, Michigan

Easy Steak Marinade

1 cup teriyaki sauce
1 cup soy sauce
1 cup Worcestershire sauce
1 cup dark rum
1 cup red wine vinegar
2 cups vegetable oil

4 tsp. extra hot horseradish
2 tsp. ground ginger
2 tsp. dry hot
   mustard
2 tsp. garlic powder

Combine all ingredients in a large jar or bowl to make marinade. Add steaks to the marinade and let soak for about 8 hours in refrigerator (or overnight). Stir occasionally to rotate the steaks. The marinade can be used 4-5 times as long as it is kept refrigerated. It can be used for any kind of meat but is especially delicious with wild game.

Chuck Crowell
Kelso, Washington

Venison and Cider Stew

2 lbs. venison, cut up for stewing
3 T. cooking oil
4 T. flour
2 tsp. salt
1 tsp. pepper
2 cups apple cider
½ cup red wine or water
2 T. vinegar

1 tsp. dried thyme
½ tsp. caraway seeds
4 carrots, cut up into large pieces
3 potatoes, peeled and cut into
   large pieces
2 onions, chopped
1 rib celery, chopped
1 apple, chopped

Combine flour, salt and pepper in small plastic or paper bag. Add meat and shake to coat. In a large pot, brown meat in hot oil. Add cider, wine and vinegar. Stir in thyme and caraway seeds. Heat until boiling, then cover, reduce heat and simmer for 1½ - 2 hours. Add vegetables and apple. Cook for ½ hour more.

Serves: 4

Tim Goles
Houston, Texas

Lazy Day Venison Lasagna

1 lb. ground venison
1 lb. uncooked lasagna noodles
1 pint cottage or ricotta cheese
1 large onion, finely chopped
1 large green pepper, finely chopped

1 lb. shredded mozzarella cheese
2 cans sliced mushrooms (or 1 cup fresh)
1 large jar prepared spaghetti sauce
salt and pepper
garlic, minced

Spray baking pan with oil and begin layering: uncooked lasagna noodles, ½ pound raw venison, ½ package cottage cheese, ½ the onion, ½ the green pepper, ½ package mozzarella cheese, 1 can mushrooms, ½ jar of spaghetti sauce, salt, pepper and garlic to taste. Continue layering until all ingredients are used.

Seal pan with foil. Bake at 350 degrees for 90 minutes. Let cool 10 minutes. You can add chopped olives, garlic chilies, layers of spinach or zucchini or anything that you want. The steam in the pan will cook the lasagna noodles.

Serves: 6

Diana Howell
Post Falls, Idaho

Perky Venison Jerky

2 lbs. venison
1 cup soy sauce
½ cup Worcestershire sauce
2 T. Tabasco sauce
1 tsp. cayenne

1 heaping tsp. ginger
1 heaping tsp. curry powder
1 heaping tsp. pepper
2 T. garlic salt
2 T. brown sugar

Mix all ingredients together and stir until sugar is dissolved. Add thinly sliced venison and marinate for 8-12 hours in refrigerator.

Preheat oven to lowest setting. lay strips in a single layer on cooking sheet and cook in oven for 12-16 hours, turning occasionally.

Yields: 36-48 strips

Ron Rodgers
Plymouth, Minnesota

Seasoned Venison Stew

1½ lbs. ground venison
2 medium potatoes, peeled and cubed
2 medium sweet potatoes, peeled and cubed
1 large onion, peeled and chopped
2 large carrots, peeled and diced
6 beef bouillon cubes
1 bay leaf
¾ tsp. fresh garlic, crushed

1 tsp. fresh black pepper
1 tsp. salt
½ tsp. red pepper
¾ tsp. marjoram
1½ tsp. parsley
1 14½-oz. can stewed tomatoes
¾ cup peas
¾ cup corn
1 heaping T. molasses

Brown meat. Put in Crockpot. Add the potatoes, sweet potatoes, onion, carrots and bouillon cubes and stir. Next add the bay leaf, garlic and dry seasonings. Pour in can stewed tomatoes, followed by peas and corn, if frozen. Add warm water until visible in pot. Top with molasses. Cover and cook on high for 1 hour.

Remove lid and stir gently until all ingredients are mixed thoroughly. Turn pot down to low and cook another 1½ hours. Serve. It's great with homemade bread.

Serves: 4

Richard Briggs
Glen Allen, Virginia

Skillet Venison Heart

1 deer heart
¼ cup Bisquick
½ tsp. salt
3 T. margarine

2 8-oz. cans mushrooms
1 10¾-oz. can chicken broth
1 tsp. instant minced onion
1 tsp. parsley flakes

Thoroughly rinse and clean heart in clean water. Chop into small pieces and shake in bag with Bisquick until coated. Melt margarine in skillet and brown heart. Add rest of ingredients, cover and simmer for 1 hour. Serve over noodles or rice.

Serves: 2

George W. Crafts, Jr.
Menasha, Wisconsin

David's Deer Stir-Fry Over Rice

2 lbs. chunked deer meat
1 stick butter
1 large red onion, chopped
1 large green pepper, chopped
1 can mushrooms, chopped
1 tsp. garlic salt
¼ tsp. black pepper
¼ tsp. seasoned salt

2½ packs brown gravymix
2 cups carrots, chopped
2 cups celery, chopped
3 cups broccoli, chopped
½ cup water chestnuts, chopped
2 cups cauliflower, chopped
2½ cups instant rice

Brown meat in ½ stick butter in wok or large nonstick pan. After meat is brown, stir in onions, green pepper, mushrooms and seasonings. After onions change color, add gravy mix and required water. Bring to a boil, then simmer on low for 10-15 minutes.

Using second half of butter, stir-fry remaining vegetables in another pan. Prepare instant rice. After vegetables are cooked to desired texture, add to meat and gravy, stir well and serve over rice in soup bowls.

Serves: 4-6

David Hoff
Perryville, Missouri

Spicy Deer Steak

deer steaks
milk
salt and pepper to taste

Grey Poupon mustard
flour
cooking oil

Soak deer steaks in milk for 10-15 minutes. Remove meat from milk and sprinkle generously with salt and pepper. Coat steaks with mustard then roll in flour and fry in deep oil until well browned.

Danny Berley
Winnsboro, South Carolina

Venison Burger Piroshkies

1 lb. ground venison
1 T. onion, chopped
2 T. green pepper, chopped
2 carrots, grated
    salt, pepper,and seasoning salt
        to taste
1 can cream of
    mushroom or cream
    of celery soup
2 cups cheese, grated
1 tube of your favorite biscuits

Fry the first four ingredients in skillet until done. Season to your taste. Stir in soup. Do not dilute with water or milk. The consistency will be thick and kind of "glued" together.

Pop open a can of biscuits (the larger ones work best), and roll one out until it is about 4-6" across. Place about ¼ cup grated cheese in middle of biscuit and spoon about ½ cup cooked burger on cheese. Depending on how large your biscuits roll out, you might have to adjust the amount of cheese and burger you put on each. Pull up the edges and pinch together tightly, then turn over and place on a cookie sheet, seam side down. Bake as directed on the biscuit package. They will puff up a bit and turn golden brown.

Serves: 4

Kristy Buck
Shelton, Washington

Venison Party Dip

1 lb. deerburger
1 lb. deer sausage
1 lb. Velveeta cheese
4 T. milk
1 12-oz. jar your favorite picante
    sauce or salsa

Brown burger and sausage in skillet. Melt cheese along with the milk in microwave. Combine burger, sausage and cheese in Crockpot with picante or salsa and simmer on high for 20 minutes.

Serve as dip with tortilla chips.

Danny Berley
Winnsboro, South Carolina

Crockpot Venison Ribs

3-4 lbs. venison ribs
½ tsp. black pepper
½ tsp. garlic powder
½ cup water
1 T. apple cider vinegar

½ cup barbecue sauce
salt to taste

Cut venison ribs into 3" x 5" pieces. Apply liberal amounts of black pepper and garlic powder. Let stand for 20 minutes. Combine ½ water and vinegar in Crockpot. Layer ribs in Crockpot and cook on medium heat for 4 hours. After 4 hours, add barbecue sauce and cook an additional 30 minutes.

Remove from Crockpot and place on serving platter. Salt to taste. Serve with broasted potatoes, garden salad and garlic toast.

Serves: 4-6

Bob Holley
Antlers, Oklahoma

Sweet and Sour Venison Stew, Crockpot Style

2 lbs. venison meat, cut up
½ cup flour
2 tsp. salt
¼ tsp. pepper
4 T. margarine
8 carrots, cut up

6 potatoes
6 stalks celery
2 cups onions, chopped
2 T. Worcestershire sauce
½ cup brown sugar
1 cup white vinegar

Mix flour, salt and pepper in bag. Add meat and shake until well coated. Brown meat in margarine in frying pan until lightly brown.

Place carrots on bottom of Crockpot, potatoes next, meat in center, celery and onions on top. Add Worcestershire sauce, brown sugar and vinegar to Crockpot on top of all ingredients. Cover and cook on low for 78 hours.

Serves: 4

Dianne M. Adams
New Milford, Connecticut

Deer Fries

2-4 lbs. venison
1 tsp. black pepper or to taste
1 tsp. onion powder
1 tsp. garlic powder
1 tsp. salt

¼ cup Worcestershire sauce
1 tsp. liquid smoke
¼ cup soy sauce
¼ cup flour

Cut meat into strips ¼" x ¼" x 4" long.

Mix all ingredients except meat, flour and cornmeal. Stir until ingredients are dissolved. Add flour and cornmeal and mix to desired thickness.

Dip meat strips in batter and drop into deep fryer for no more than 30-45 seconds or until starting to brown. Best served hot or warm.

Yields: Appetizer for a large group

Randall Breshears
Moberly, Missouri

Cheesy Tomato Venison Steak

1 lb. cubed deer steak
    salt and pepper
¼ cup flour
1 T. oil
1 T. butter

¼ cup flour
1 can stewed tomatoes
1 T. Worcestershire sauce
¾ cup cheese, grated

Season and flour steak. Brown in oil and remove meat (leave drippings in pan). Butter a 9" x 12" pan and arrange browned meat in a single layer.

In pan, combine flour with drippings. Next, pour in tomatoes and Worcestershire sauce and stir as mixture is heated. Allow to thicken a little while cooking for 2-3 minutes.

Pour mixture over meat and cover with foil. Bake at 325 degrees for 1½ hours. When ready to serve, sprinkle grated cheese over meat and allow to melt.

Serves: 4

Danny Berley
Winnsboro, South Carolina

Hot Stuff Chili

4 lbs. ground venison	1 jar jalapeno peppers, pickled
1 lb. beans, dried (red, pinto or both)	1 T. black pepper
4-6 onions	1 T. red pepper
1 clove garlic	1 T. chili powder
1 small can tomato paste	1 T. crushed dried red peppers
1 large can tomato sauce	3 T. oregano
1 4½-oz. can green chilies, chopped	1 bottle ketchup (optional)

Boil beans in large pot of water for about 2 hours. Brown meat and drain.

Peel and finely chop onions and garlic. Add to beans and simmer about 1 more hour. Add remaining ingredients except ketchup and simmer over low heat for 1 more hour. Stir chili often so it doesn't burn on bottom of pot. Add ketchup for extra tomato flavor, if desired.

You can't cook chili too long. The longer it simmers, the more the spices blend. Vary ingredients and amounts to your own taste. Experiment. Good chili is never made exactly the same way twice.

Serves: 8

Dan E. Drake
Hoagland, Indiana

Venison Jerky

1-2 lbs. venison, thinly sliced	1 heaping tsp. ginger
1 cup soy sauce	1 heaping tsp. curry powder
1 cup Worcestershire sauce	1 heaping tsp. pepper
1 cup tomato sauce	2 heaping tsp. garlic salt

For marinade, mix all ingredients except meat and stir well. Marinate venison in mixture in refrigerator for 8-12 hours.

Heat oven on lowest setting and bake until leathery. Or use food dehydrator.

Yields: 24-36 jerky strips

Dan E. Drake
Hoagland, Indiana

Swiss Style Venison Steak

6-8 deer steaks, trimmed
    flour
    pepper
3 T. cooking oil
1 cup red wine
1 large yellow onion, chopped
1 large green bell pepper, chopped

1 whole glove garlic, chopped
1 qt. stewed tomatoes
1 tsp. oregano
1 tsp. basil
12 oz. fresh mushrooms, sliced

Mix flour and pepper in resealable plastic bag, add steaks and shake. Brown steaks in skillet with oil. Drain excess oil.

Add all other ingredients except mushrooms and cook on medium heat for 20-30 minutes. Add mushrooms 10 minutes before serving. Excellent served over rice or noodles.

Serves: 6-8

Frank Albert
Manteca, California

Slow Cooked Venison

1 venison roast
2 T. olive oil
1 large Spanish onion, sliced
    salt and pepper

Fry roast in oil until browned all over.

Cover with sliced onion and sprinkle with salt and pepper to taste.

Add water to cover bottom of pan ¼". Simmer over very low heat until water is almost gone. Add more water and continue simmering. Repeat this step until meat is very tender, usually about 2 hours.

Once meat is tender, allow most of water to cook off. Add more salt and pepper if desired and serve.

Serves: 4-6 (depending on size of roast)

Frank Kurant, Jr.
Rutland, Utah

Deer Roast

1 deer roast	1 envelope onion soup or beefy
celery salt to taste	onion soup
3-4 cloves garlic	2 jars ready-made beef gravy
1 small can mushrooms	1 bay leaf
1 can golden mushroom soup	

Put all ingredients in roaster. Cook at 350 degrees for 3 hours. Add water if needed to prevent burning or cook in large oven bag.

Serves: 4-6 (depending on size of roast)

Jerry Baylor
Leechburg, Pennsylvania

Charlie's Special Venison Meat Balls

2 lb. venison hamburger	¼ tsp. pepper
2 eggs	½ tsp. garlic powder
⅓ cup ketchup	1 T. soy sauce
1¼ cups oatmeal, dry	½ cup onions, chopped

Mix all ingredients, roll into meatballs and put in 9" x 13" pan.

Sauce

2 T. brown sugar
1 T. lemon juice
1 12-oz. bottle chili sauce
1 can jellied cranberry sauce

In small saucepan, heat and mix until hot and smooth. Pour over meat balls and bake at 350 degrees for 30 minutes.

Yields: 24 meatballs

Charles M. Robinson
St. Maries, Indiana

Sunday Venison and Raspberry Sauce

1 deer backstrap (loin)
   salt, pepper and other favorite seasonings
½ lb. pork sausage
2 cups fresh mushrooms, sliced
2 leeks, thinly sliced
3 cups spinach, chopped

Cut backstrap to about 12" long. Make 2 cuts ¾ through down full length. Pound flat to about ½" to ¾" thick. Rub with seasoning on one side.

Brown sausage and remove meat from skillet, leaving fat. Add mushrooms and leeks. Cook until mushrooms are tender. Drain excess fat. Add spinach and cover. Cook until spinach is wilted.

Place mixture in center of flattened backstrap. Roll or pull up edges (lengthwise) and secure with toothpicks or butcher's twine. Place on rack in covered dish and bake in oven at 350 degrees for 4050 minutes.

Raspberry Sauce

¼ cup white onion, finely minced
¼ stick butter or margarine
½ cup raspberries
½ cup cranberries

In small saucepan, cook onion in butter until onion is clear. Add berries and mash. Cover saucepan and cook until berry mixture thickens, about 30 minutes. If berries do not thicken, add 1 tsp. cornstarch in 1 oz. cold water and stir.

To serve, place venison on platter and slice into ¼" to ½" medallions. (They resemble swirl cookies.) Drizzle sauce over medallions.

Baked winter squash makes an excellent companion dish.

Serves: 4

Charles Warriner
Pine Bluff, Arkansas

Terri's Venison Stew

1½ lbs. venison round, cut into 1" cubes
1 cup red wine vinegar
1 cup water
3 T. flour
3 T. cooking oil
1 medium onion, sliced
3 cloves fresh garlic, chopped
⅓ cup red wine
6 potatoes, cut into 1" chunks
1 1lb. bag peeled baby carrots
2 packets brown seasoning mix
¼ cup gravy master
3 bay leaves
1 10oz. box frozen peas
  salt and pepper to taste

Soak venison cubes overnight in vinegar and water mixture. Drain and rinse venison. Put venison and flour in plastic bag and shake until coated.

Heat oil in large frying pan or Dutch oven. Brown venison, onion and garlic about 10 minutes. Add red wine. Cover and simmer for 5 minutes.

Add potatoes, carrots, brown seasoning mix, gravy master, bay leaves, peas, salt and pepper. Cover with water and bring to a boil. Cover and simmer about 1½ hours. Serve over white rice or noodles.

Serves: 4-6

Terri Zayat
Leonia, New Jersey

Wyoming Venison Jerky

1 lb. venison meat, cut into thin strips for smoking
1 8 oz. hickory smoke barbecue sauce
1½ tsp. Worcestershire sauce
1 tsp. soy sauce
1 T. garlic chili pepper sauce
3 cups water
10 oz. Heinz 57 Sauce
1 T. white or black pepper
½ tsp. salt
½ tsp. onion salt
3 T. ketchup

Mix ingredients with meat. Allow meat to absorb sauce for 1 day in refrigerator. Stir occasionally.

Place meat on smoker or dehydrator until done.

Yields: 18-24 pieces

Josh Hatch
Evanston, Wyoming

Kent's Hot Deer Jerky

2 lbs. venison, thinly sliced
1½ cups soy sauce
¼ cup liquid smoke
¼ cup Worcestershire sauce
2 T. brown sugar
1 T. garlic salt
2 T. black pepper
2 T. red pepper, crushed

Place all ingredients except meat in a bowl and mix well. Add meat and let soak for 2 hours. Drain.

Place strips of meat in a dehydrator. Let dehydrate for about 16 hours or until meat is completely dry but not crunchy.

Yields: 24-36 jerky strips

Penny and Kent Lambert
Hiddenite, North Carolina

Ray's Camp Stew

5 lbs. venison, cut in 1" cubes
3 T. oil
½ lb. onions, cut in ¾" pieces
½ lb. celery
3 cloves garlic
½ cup flour
1 qt. water or stock, boiling
1 pint canned tomatoes, chopped
2 12-oz. cans beer
1 tsp. dried thyme
2 bay leaves
1 tsp. ground pepper
1 T. salt
2 tsp. Worcestershire sauce
½ lb. carrots, peeled and
  cut in ¾" pieces
1 lb. potatoes, peeled and cut in
  ¾" pieces

Brown venison cubes in oil in heavy pot. Remove cubes, leaving oil. Add onions, celery and garlic and cook until tender.

Sprinkle flour in pot, stirring well. Gradually add boiling water or stock; stir until thick and smooth. Add tomatoes, beer, spices, Worcestershire sauce and venison. Stir until well mixed. Reduce heat and simmer, uncovered, for 1 hour and 15 minutes, stirring occasionally. Add carrots and cook 30 minutes more, covered. Add potatoes and cook until they are tender.

Serves: 12-15

Ray Miller, Jr.
Bradford, Pennsylvania

Okie Roast Venison

4 lb. venison roast
2 cloves fresh garlic, slivered
1 16-oz. cola
1 tsp. seasoning salt
4 medium onions, peeled

Cut narrow slits in meat and place pieces of garlic in them, getting as deep as you can. Place meat in resealable plastic bag. Pour soda into bag, add seasoning salt and let marinate over night or at least 6-8 hours. Drain meat and cook, covered, until tender and brown.

Billy R. Estep
Newalla, Oklahoma

Randy's Whoo Chili

2 lbs. ground venison
1 16-oz. jar chili mix
1 4½-oz. can mushrooms, whole or sliced, drained
1 16-oz. can hot chili beans
1½ T. chili powder
1 tsp. black pepper
1 T. Worcestershire sauce
1 tsp. salt
1 T. liquid smoke
2 cloves garlic, minced
1 large onion, chopped
1 16-oz. tomato juice
1 15-oz. can crushed tomatoes

Brown meat with onion and garlic and drain. Combine all remaining ingredients in Crockpot. Cover and cook 8-10 hours on low or 4-5 hours on high. Stir 2-3 times.

Serves: 6-8

Randy White
Wenona, Illinois

Deer Bar-B-Que Meatballs

3 lb. ground venison
1 12-oz. can evaporated milk
1 cup oatmeal, dry
1 cup cracker crumbs
2 eggs
½ cup onions, chopped
½ tsp. garlic powder
2 tsp. chili powder

Combine all ingredients. Mixture will be soft. Shape into walnut-sized balls. Put in single layer on waxed paper-lined cookie sheet. Freeze until solid. Store in resealable plastic bags until ready to cook. When ready to eat meatballs, prepare a sauce as follows:

Sauce

2 cups ketchup
1 cup brown sugar
½ tsp. liquid smoke or to taste
½ tsp. garlic powder
¼ cup onion, chopped

Combine all ingredients. Stir until sugar dissolves. Put meatballs in cooking bowl. Pour sauce over and bake at 350 degrees for 1 hour.

Yields: 70-80 meatballs

Jerry Baylor
Leechburg, Pennsylvania

Arabian Stew

2 lbs. venison stew meat
2 T. cooking oil
1 16-oz. can sliced stewed tomatoes
1½ cups celery, diced
1 cup onions, diced

1 cup rice, cooked until almost done
   salt, pepper and garlic salt
2 16-oz. cans water
   (or more if needed)

Brown venison in cooking oil. Add tomatoes and simmer 10-15 minutes to help tenderize meat.

Add celery and onions. Cook 10-15 minutes. Add water, rice and seasonings to taste. Cook until done, about 20 minutes, stirring occasionally.

Serves: 4

Dennis Blomberg
Hurley, Wisconsin

Bracchioli in Tomato and White Wine Sauce

2 lb. deer rump roast
3 cloves garlic, minced
1 tsp. grated Parmesan cheese
1 tsp. parsley

2 T. olive oil
1 small onion, diced
1 cup dry white Italian table wine
1 pint whole canned tomatoes

Pound meat with mallet to ¼" thickness. Sprinkle with garlic, Parmesan cheese and parsley. Fold the sides over ¼" to form a pocket and roll from the bottom up with the crease side down. Thread a toothpick through the center.

Pour olive oil into a large saucepan over medium heat. Saute onion, then brown meat. When meat is browned, add white wine. Cook in wine for 5 minutes and then add tomatoes. Cover and simmer for 30 minutes, stirring juice and flipping meat over once during cooking.

Serves: 4

Don Gentile
Paulsboro, New Jersey

Venison Heart Casserole

1 venison heart
1 4-oz. can mushrooms
1 small onion, sliced thin
¼ lb. margarine
1 tsp. salt

2 tsp. pepper
2 tsp. minced garlic
½ cup red wine
sprinkle of basil

Trim heart of all connective tissue and dice. Marinate in milk overnight or at least 4 hours. Strain meat, melt margarine in casserole, add all ingredients and stir. Sprinkle with basil.

Cover and bake at 350 degrees for 40 minutes. Soak up the juices with warm french bread or hard rolls.

Serves: 2

Joe Russo
Coaldale, Colorado

Venison Tenderloins

4-6 venison tenderloin steaks, cut 1" thick
½ stick butter
2 T. olive oil
½ yellow onion, chopped
1 garlic clove, minced
  salt and pepper to taste
  tarragon Dijon mustard

Melt butter in large saucepan on medium-low heat. Add olive oil, onion and garlic to pan and saute. Add venison steaks and salt and pepper to your liking and cook for 3-4 minutes (depending on how rare you like your meat). Turn steaks and add a dab of tarragon Dijon mustard on each piece. Cook 1-2 minutes, flip and cook on other side. Place steaks on large serving dish and scoop remaining sauce over meat and garnish with sprigs of tarragon or rosemary.

Serves: 4-6

Bill Browne
Aliso Viejo, California

Deer Fondue

2 lbs. deer meat
2 cups burgundy, sherry or Port wine
   (or your favorite red wine)
2 cups beef broth
2 small garlic cloves, chopped fine

1 tsp. pepper
1 tsp. dill weed
1 tsp. thyme
½ cup olive or peanut oil

Cut deer meat in ½" cubes. Use lean cuts with all fat and connective tissue removed.

Mix remaining ingredients, add to fondue pot and bring to a slow, gentle boil. Skewer meat and cook in fondue pot until well done. Serve with your favorite dips, such as garlic butter or sour cream and onion dip.

Serves: 4

Robert Daerr
Brooklyn, Ohio

Cajun Deer Steaks

2 lbs. deer steaks
⅓ cup chopped green bell pepper
⅓ cup chopped yellow bell pepper
⅓ cup chopped red bell pepper
3 T. fresh chopped parsley
3 T. fresh chopped chives
1 T. lemon juice

½ tsp. salt
½ tsp. cayenne pepper
1 medium onion, chopped
1 clove garlic, crushed
1 28-oz. can whole tomatoes,
   chopped, with juice
3 cups hot, cooked rice

Heat oven to 450 degrees. Place steaks in 11" x 7" x 1½" baking dish, ungreased. Mix remaining ingredients except rice. Pour over steaks. Bake, uncovered for 25-30 minutes, spooning tomato mixture over steaks occasionally. Serve over rice.

Serves: 4-6

Jim Hall
Fort Wayne, Indiana

White Tail Texas Deer Chili

2½ lb. deer meat
1 lb. ground lean pork
½ lb. pinto beans
5 cups canned tomatoes
1 lb. chopped green peppers
1½ T. salad oil
1½ lbs. chopped onions
2 cloves crushed garlic

½ cup chopped parsley
½ cup butter
½ cup chili powder
2 T. salt
1½ tsp. pepper
1½ tsp. cumin seed
1½ tsp. MSG

Wash beans and put in a saucepan. Add enough water to cover the beans by 2 inches. Soak overnight. Bring to a boil, reduce heat and simmer in same water until done, do not drain. Add tomatoes and simmer for 5 minutes.

Saute green peppers in salad oil for 5 minutes. Add onions and cook until tender, stirring often. Add garlic and parsley.

Melt butter in large skillet and saute venison and pork for 15 minutes. Add meat to green pepper and onion mixture, stir in chili powder and cook 10 minutes. Add this to the beans and spices. Simmer covered for 1 hour then cook uncovered for 30 more minutes.

Serves: 8

Gene Prickette
Waco, Texas

Crockpot Venison Tips

3 lb. venison roast, cut into tips
  salt and pepper to taste
1 pkg. dried onion soup mix

1 can cream of mushroom soup
1 can mushrooms, drained

Rinse and dry venison. Salt and pepper and place in Crockpot. Mix soups together and pour over venison. Cook on low-medium for 6-8 hours. Add mushrooms during last hour and water if needed to keep from drying. Serve over hot noodles.

Serves: 8

Michael D. Ryan
Coraopolis, Pennsylvania

Venison Cabbage Rolls

1 lb. ground venison
1 tsp. Cajun seasoning
1 tsp. garlic salt
1 egg

¼ cup long grain rice
3 T. red wine
1 head cabbage, cored

Combine all ingredients, except cabbage, and set aside.

Blanch cabbage. Peel leaves off carefully. Place ¼ cup of venison mixture in center of each large cabbage leaf. Roll each leaf, folding sides around meat mixture. Place a toothpick through edges of leaves to hold them together in a roll.

Place in a 2" baking pan and bake at 350 degrees for 45-60 minutes. While cabbage rolls are cooking, you can make the sauce.

2 8-oz. cans tomato sauce
1½ T. basil
1 tsp. garlic salt

Mix ingredients together in a saucepan and let simmer. When done, place cabbage rolls on plates, then lace the tops with the basil sauce. Makes a sweet but spicy combination.

Serves: 4-6

Michelle Cline
Reedley, California

*C*HEF *JOHN SCHUMACHER* is a life-long hunter and a Life Member of the North American Hunting Club. He's also the owner of Schumachers Historic European Hotel and Restaurant in New Prague, Minnesota. Schumachers is a world famous country inn and is well-known for its delicious game dinners.

Chef John has made a career of preparing food people love, so you can be sure he's developed some tempting wild game dishes...especially his favorite, venison.

We asked the chef to share some of his favorite venison recipes with other NAHC Members. After much thought, he finally came up with the ones he likes to prepare for family and friends. Then he invited a few staff members down to his home and prepared them for us all in one afternoon.

We had a great time, ate like pigs and still anticipated each new dish as he served it. You'll love these, too!

Kabobs

16 1" cubes of venison
1 pint herb-flavored bottled dressing
8 jumbo mushrooms
1 cup sherry wine
8 pearl onions or shallots
8 2" pieces red or green pepper
8 cubes fresh melon (honeydew or cantaloupe)
8 slices zucchini, ¼" thick

Place venison cubes in a glass or stainless steel bowl. Cover with herb dressing and refrigerate for approximately 72 hours.

Cut stems from mushrooms and simmer in sherry wine until tender. Remove liquid and keep. Set mushrooms aside. Peel and blanch onions in 1 quart salted water until tender. Drain liquid and set aside.

Bring 1 quart salted water to boil. Add peppers. When water returns to a boil, remove the peppers and set aside. Remove skin from melon and cut into large cubes.

Place items on skewers in the following order: mushroom, onion, meat, red or green pepper, zucchini, meat, melon, meat, zucchini, red/green pepper, meat, onion, mushroom.

Place on a medium grill (not too hot). Grill until meat and vegetables are done to your liking. While grilling, combine 1 cup meat marinade and liquid from the mushrooms and baste over the skewers.

Use any game or red meat. Use any vegetables you like. Precook them first. Use your imagination.

Serves: 4

Venison Stroganoff

12 pieces sliced venison, 1-2 oz. each
1 cup flour
½ tsp. salt
¼ tsp. white pepper
¼ cup butter
½ cup shallots or red onions

⅔ cup sherry wine
2 cups brown gravy
1 cup sour cream
8 fresh large mushrooms

Remove all fat and silver skin from venison. Flatten with a meat mallet. Place flour, salt and white pepper in a pie plate and mix to combine. Place meat slices into flour and coat. Shake off excess flour. Set aside.

Place butter in a large frying pan and bring to a fast bubble. Add shallots and cook until clear. Add game slices and cook for 2 minutes. Turn and cook other side for 2 minutes.

Add sherry, gravy, sour cream and mushrooms . Simmer on low heat for 10 minutes. Serve with rice, wild rice or egg noodles.

Serves: 4

Venison Pancakes

2 lbs. venison
1 lb. bulk pork sausage
1 tsp. salt
1 tsp. black pepper

1 tsp. thyme
2 cloves garlic, minced
⅓ cup fresh bread crumbs
1 beaten egg

Grind chilled venison (grinds best when almost frozen). Place in a bowl and add remaining ingredients. Mix well to combine.

Rub your hands with flour and then form 8 venison patties. Pan fry slowly until patties are cooked thoroughly. Drain off the fat as the patties cook. Applesauce is a nice accompaniment to these venison pancakes.

Hint: You can vary the taste of these pancakes by changing the kinds of sausage you use.

Serves: 8

Venison Zucchini Boats

1 lb. ground venison
1 T. olive oil
2 cups onion, diced fine
4 zucchini, each about
    6-8 inches long
1 T. Worcestershire sauce
½ tsp. black pepper

2 cups shredded sharp
    Cheddar cheese
2 cups shredded Swiss Cheese
½ cup Parmesan cheese
2 fresh Jalapeno peppers,
    sliced (optional)

In a heavy pan, cook venison and onions in oil until venison is done and onions are tender. Drain off the fat.

Wash zucchini and cut in half lengthwise. Remove seeds by scraping with a teaspoon, making a trench in the middle of each zucchini half, leaving ½" on either end. Brush with Worcestershire sauce and sprinkle with black pepper. Fill zucchini halves evenly with the venison/onion mixture and top with Cheddar and Swiss cheeses. Spread a few pepper slices over cheese and sprinkle Parmesan on top. Bake in oven at 400 degrees until cheese is melted and crisp. Serve hot, in whole or 2" pieces.

Serves: 4-6

Venison Stir Fry

3 cups venison strips, 2 x ¼"
    (fat and silver skin removed)
¼ cup olive oil
3 cloves garlic
1 cup carrots
½ cup celery
1 cup fresh mushrooms, sliced thick
½ cup red peppers, diced in large pieces

½ tsp. black pepper
½ cup red onions, sliced
2 tomatoes, cut in 8 wedges
1 T. Worcestershire sauce
1 tsp. soy sauce

In a heavy pan, heat olive oil until almost smoking. Add meat and cook until browned. Push meat to one side. Add garlic, vegetables and black pepper and cook for 5 minutes, stirring to keep from sticking. Add Worcestershire sauce and soy sauce and stir. Cook until vegetables are tender. Serve with noodles, rice or wild rice.

Serves: 6-8

Venison Steak Brown Beer Soup

    4 cups venison
    ¼ cup vegetable oil
    1½ cups summer squash
    1½ cups onions, diced ½" thick
    1½ cups carrots, diced ½" thick
    1½ cups celery
    1½ cups potatoes, peeled and
         diced ½" thick
    2 cloves garlic
    ½ cup A-1 Steak Sauce
    1 cup wild rice
    1 T. beef base
    1 tsp. black pepper
    3 cups dark beer
    3 bay leaves
    6 cups water
    1 tsp. allspice

It is most important to remove all silver skin and fat from the venison. Cut into strips ½" thick and 2" long. Heat oil to smoke hot. Add venison and brown, stirring with a wooden spoon.

When venison is brown, remove to a strainer to drain off liquid. Place all ingredients in a slow cooker on high and cook 5 hours.

Serves: 8

Big Game

Antelope
Bear
Boar

Caribou
Elk
Moose
Sheep

Robert E. Hyde, Jr.

Elk Swiss Steak

2-3 lbs. elk round steak
  1 T. margarine
  1 large onion, sliced
    flour

Roll steak pieces in flour and brown in margarine. Put steak in slow cooker and layer with onion, soup mix, and mushroom soup. Sprinkle with garlic salt to taste. Cook until tender. Remove steak and thicken sauce for gravy.

Serves: 4-6

Robert E. Hyde, Jr.
Greenville, Michigan

Wild Pig California Style

3-4 lbs. boneless wild pig meat,
    cut in strips
2 cans cold beer
1 large onion, thinly sliced and
    rings separated

¼ cup chopped cilantro
juice of one lime

In a bowl, layer the onions, pork and cilantro. Pour the cold beer and lime juice over the top. Stir the meat slightly to be sure the beer thoroughly penetrates the layers. Marinate in refrigerator for 1-4 hours, stirring occasionally.

10 flour tortillas
6 tomatillos, chopped
1 onion, chopped
2 tomatoes, chopped

1 ripe avocado, chopped
chili peppers, chopped
cilantro, chopped

Grill the meat and onion slices on a hot barbecue, cooking until well done, but still moist. Remove to a plate and serve with warmed tortillas and the chopped ingredients.

Lay out a tortilla on your plate with some pork in the middle. Then add desired ingredients, roll it up and eat. Refried beans with a little grated cheese is a traditional side dish.

Serves: 4-6

Ron North
San Clemente, California

Ferguson Stew

1 lb. cubed moose meat	2 beef bouillon cubes
½ cup flour	1 large green pepper, diced
½ tsp. salt	½ tsp. parsley
¼ tsp. pepper	1 large onion, diced
2 T. cooking oil	¼ tsp. thyme
6 cups water	1 T. salt
5-6 medium potatoes, cubed	1 cup cold water
6-8 carrots, cut up	2 T. cornstarch
3-4 celery stalks, cut up	

Mix flour, ½ tsp. salt and pepper in bowl. Coat meat with flour mixture and brown in Dutch oven in cooking oil. Add any leftover flour mixture to meat after browning. Add water and simmer for 2 hours.

Add vegetables, bouillon, salt and seasonings. Cook for 1 hour more or until veggies are done. To thicken, mix cold water and cornstarch together and add to stew. Bring to a boil and stir for 3 minutes. Great with homemade biscuits.

Serves: 4

Heather L. Ferguson
Mattawamkeag, Maine

Crockpot Smoked Game Roast

1 game roast
¼ cup liquid smoke
½ tsp. celery salt
½ tsp. garlic salt
½ tsp. onion salt

Lay roast on large piece of foil. Pour liquid smoke over roast and add salts. Wrap tightly in 2 layers of foil. Place in Crockpot. Cook on low 8-12 hours. Foil keeps all liquid around roast and will be very moist.

Serves: 6-8

David W. Harris
Osage, Minnesota

Ram Arm Roast

1 roast of ram arm
  salt and pepper to taste
1 tsp. garlic powder
1 T. Lawry's Seasoned Salt

1 pkg. dried onion soup mix
water
cornstarch (as needed)

Rinse and drain roast. Add salt, pepper, garlic powder, and Lawry's Seasoned Salt to both sides of meat. Place in roaster and sprinkle roast with onion soup mix. Add water on side of meat in roaster (not on top of meat) to almost cover meat. Roast at 300 - 350 degrees for 3 hours or until tender. Thicken gravy with cornstarch.

Serves: 4-6

Gary Breitwieser
Cuzco, Indiana

Elk Stew

2 lbs. elk tenderloin, cubed
1 cup unbleached flour
½ cup vegetable oil or margarine
1 large white onion, sliced
2 medium russet potatoes, cut up
3 large washed carrots, cut up
2 cups cold water

1 pkg. pork gravy mix
1 pkg. au jus mix
¼ cup barbecue sauce
1 cup tomato juice
3 T. Tabasco sauce
2 T. black pepper

In Crockpot, put in cold water, pork and au jus mixes, barbecue sauce, tomato juice, Tabasco sauce and pepper. Heat on high temperature.

In frying pan, heat oil on medium temperature until hot. Put flour in a resealable plastic bag, add meat and shake until coated. Put in frying pan and brown on all sides.

Add browned elk to Crockpot along with vegetables and cook on high heat until potatoes and carrots are tender.

Serve with any type of crusty bread and butter. A nice Merlot wine will go great with this dish.

Serves: 6-8

Keith Olsen
Hoffman Estates, Illinois

"Hickory Sticks" Sweet and Sour Mountain Lion Sausage Meatballs

1 lb. mountain lion sausage
1 cup flour
1 tsp. salt
1 tsp. garlic
1 tsp. pepper
¼ cup chopped dried parsley flakes
1 T. cooking oil

Roll sausage into medium sized meat balls. Mix flour, salt, garlic, pepper and parsley flakes. Roll meat balls generously in flour mixture and fry in oil until browned on all sides. Remove from fry pan, drain on paper towels and place in an oven-safe dish or pan.

2 cups chopped celery
1 medium onion, chopped
1 medium green pepper, chopped
1 #1 can sliced mushrooms
1 stick margarine
1 #2 can crushed pineapple, with juice

2 T. cornstarch
6 T. vinegar
2 T. soy sauce

Mix vegetables, mushrooms and margarine together in a glass bowl and cook 10 minutes in microwave on high. Add pineapple. Bring to a boil.

Combine the cornstarch, vinegar, soy sauce and apricot preserves. Stir to blend well. Add to vegetable/pineapple mixture, and stir until thickened. Pour over browned meat balls. Bake for 1 hour at 350 degrees.

Serve on rice or noodles.

Serves: 6-8

John L. Cripe
Sagle, Idaho

Vernel Wagner

Marinated Mountain Goat Steaks

4 steaks, 1" thick
¼ cup hickory, apple, cherry or plum wood chips soaked in water for
    one hour, drained.

Marinade

1 clove garlic, mashed or ⅛ tsp.
    garlic powder
⅓ cup low-salt soy sauce
⅓ cup dry cooking wine

¼ cup honey or 1 tsp. sesame oil
1 T. lemon or lime juice or cider vinegar
    (optional)

Mix all marinade ingredients together. Pierce the steaks several times with a fork. This will allow the marinade to absorb into the meat. Put marinade an steaks in a resealable plastic bag and marinate meat for 24 hours in the refrigerator, shaking bag often.

Start grill and place soaked chips on the coals or lava rock. When the grill is hot and the chips are smoking, grill the steaks until medium rare to medium well to have tender, moist meat. If the meat is cooked until well done, it will be tough and dry. Of course, smoking the meat is optional. It's just as good with the smoke as without.

Serves: 4

Vernel Wagner
Big Timber, Montana

Wild Burritos

1 game roast
  salt and pepper to taste
1 tsp. garlic powder
½ tsp. cayenne pepper (optional)
  flour tortillas
  lettuce, shredded
  tomatoes, chopped
  cheese, grated
  onion, minced
  sour cream
  guacamole
  chilies, chopped

Sear a roast on all sides (any wild red meat) in hot skillet after seasoning with salt, pepper and garlic powder. If you like it spicy, also add cayenne.

Place in a Crockpot on low setting all day or overnight. Meat will be very tender. Shred meat. Place meat lengthwise on top of flour tortilla. Add lettuce, tomatoes, cheese, onion, sour cream, guacamole, chilies or any other combo of your choice. Roll up and enjoy!

Serves: 8

Rodney H. Erickson, P.A.
Eagle Point, Oregon

Moose Stew

1½ lbs. moose, cubed
1 T. margarine
2 medium onions, sliced
2 quarts water
1 medium turnip, chopped
2 celery stalks, chopped
3 medium white potatoes, chopped
3 carrots, cut up
3 cloves garlic, minced
5 bay leaves
½ tsp. crushed red pepper

Melt margarine in a 5-6 quart pan. Brown meat and onion over medium heat. Add water and boil for 1 hour. Add vegetables, garlic, bay leaves and red pepper. Simmer for 1-2 hours, until meat is tender. Add salt and pepper to taste.

Serves: 4-6

Carolyn Bickford
Peru, Maine

Gourmet Big Game

1 small game roast
1 T. olive oil
2 garlic cloves, slivered

½ cup of your favorite marinade
3 T. apricot preserves
1 T. lemon pepper

Marinate roast 3-4 hours in a resealable bag. Reserve marinade. Make small cuts in sides and top of roast. Insert garlic slivers.

Preheat frying pan to 325 degrees. Brown roast on all sides in olive oil. Turn heat down to simmer. Combine reserved marinade with apricot preserves and lemon pepper. Pour mixture over roast. Simmer until meat is spongy when pressed with a finger. Cooking any longer will make it tough. The remainder of the "drippings" can be put over rice or potatoes.

Serves: 4

Jerry Cernollavek
Laurel, Montana

Oven Baked Bear Steaks

1½ lbs. bear steak
1 cup red cooking wine
1 T. Worcestershire sauce
1 T. soy sauce
1 tsp. meat tenderizer
¼ tsp. minced garlic
¼ tsp. ground pepper

4 stalks celery, cut in half
1 envelope beefy mushroom soup mix
½ onion, cut into pieces
2 cups water
2 cups potatoes, cut into 1" cubes
1 8-oz. sliced fresh mushrooms

Marinate steak in wine, Worcestershire sauce, soy sauce, meat tenderizer, garlic and pepper for 1-3 hours. Drain off marinade and place steak in roasting pan on top of celery pieces. Add soup mix envelope, water and onion. Bake covered in roasting pan at 350 degrees for 3 hours. Add potatoes and mushrooms during last 45 minutes of baking.

Serves: 4

Karen Witman
N. Irwin, Pennsylvania

Grilled Buffalo Tongue

1 buffalo tongue
pepper, seasoned salt and garlic powder to taste

Boil buffalo tongue in water for approximately 1½ hours. Remove and put in cold water for a few minutes to stop cooking process. Peel the skin off. Season to taste with pepper, seasoned salt and garlic powder.

Place on grill over medium coals for approximately 15-20 minutes, turning to roast all sides. If you like a smokier taste, add some hickory chips to the coals.

Slice and serve with salad vegetables. Also great on sandwiches or cheese crackers.

Serves: 4-6

T. (Dog Face) Silagi
Orangevale, California

Moose Chili

2 lbs. ground moose meat	¼ cup chili powder
1 large onion, chopped	1 tsp. garlic powder
1 whole jalapeno pepper, chopped	1 tsp. salt
1 large can tomatoes	1 T. cumin powder
2 cans kidney beans	1 T. paprika

Brown moose meat with onions. Add remaining ingredients and cook slowly for 1 hour.

Serves: 8

Jack and Sarah Adams
Jay, Oklahoma

Jack Adams

Moose Steaks in Mushroom Gravy

2 lbs. moose steak	1 can cream of mushroom soup and 1 can water
2 T. cooking oil	salt and pepper to taste

Salt and pepper steaks. Heat skillet, add oil and cook steaks until meat is browned. Add mushroom soup and water. Cook slowly for 15-20 minutes.

Serves: 4

Jack and Sarah Adams
Jay, Oklahoma

Simple Big Game Corned Meat

Stir together thoroughly in a large pot:

2 quarts water
1 cup salt
1 T. Italian seasoning
1 tsp. mixed pickle spice
1 clove garlic, crushed with salt
2 tsp. pepper
¼ tsp. saltpeter (optional)

Add:

Large, boned game roast (4-6 pounds)

Place a heavy object on meat to keep it under water. Cover pot and for 48 hours or more. Leaving meat in brine longer will get the middle more pink. Remove from brine, wash and tie meat to keep the shape.

In separate pot, cover meat with cold water. Bring to a boil. Remove scum, cover and simmer 4-5 hours. Skim at intervals. Let cool.

Serve with horseradish or Honey Orange Glaze:

½ cup honey
1 cup brown sugar, packed
½ cup orange juice

Mix together and heat. Pour over meat to serve.

Serves: 8-12

Nancy Swanson
Kalispell, Montana

Rowdy's Teriyaki Pie

2 lbs. ground game meat (deer, elk, bear or antelope)
2 slices bacon
1 cup sliced carrots
3 medium potatoes, cubed
½ cup onion, chopped
2 cups Teriyaki sauce
   salt and pepper to taste

In large bowl, mix ground meat, carrots, potatoes and onions and 1½ cups of the Teriyaki sauce. Mix well and put into an 8" x 11" baking dish. Lay bacon over meat mixture and pour the rest of the Teriyaki sauce on top, then cover with pie crust.

Pie crust

1¼ cups flour
½ tsp. salt
½ cup shortening
½ cup milk

Stir together flour and salt. Cut in shortening until pieces are the size of small peas. Pour in milk and mix until all is moistened and will form a ball. Roll out to size and shape of your cooking bowl.

After covering meat with pie crust, brush with egg wash (1 egg and pinch of salt). This will give pie a brown glazed look. Bake at 350 degrees for 2 1/2 hours.

Serves: 6-8

Mike Enderle
Cape Girardeau, Missouri

Marcus McNew

Caribou Goulash (Bou Gou)

1 lb. ground caribou
½ cup chopped onion
1 small can mushrooms, drained
3 cloves garlic, chopped
1 large can Italian style stewed
    tomatoes, drained
    salt and pepper to taste

2 15-oz. cans tomato sauce
1 small can tomato paste
½ tsp. ground oregano
3 bay leaves
1 T. basil leaves
1 22-oz. bag of elbow macaroni
    noodles

Brown caribou burger in a cast iron skillet. Drain grease. Add onions, mushrooms, garlic, salt and pepper and cook 15-30 minutes on medium heat until the ingredients are cooked into the meat.

In a 2 quart sauce pan, mix stewed tomatoes, tomato sauce, tomato paste, oregano, bay leaves, basil leaves and meat mixture. Mix thoroughly and simmer for 1½ - 2 hours on low heat.

Boil noodles until done. Rinse thoroughly with hot water. Mix meat sauce with noodles, stir and enjoy your Bou Gou!

Serves: 4

Marcus McNew
Murdock, Minnesota

Elk Tenderloins

4 elk tenderloins
½ cup flour
2 cloves garlic, chopped

2 T. butter
salt and pepper to taste

Cut loins into 2" steaks. Stand steak on edge and butterfly it by cutting it ⅔ of the way through. Roll in salt, pepper and flour.

Heat frying pan to very hot temperature. Drop garlic and butter into pan and after heating for a few seconds, add meat. Sear meat on each side. Searing is a cooking method that quickly cooks the outside of the meat, sealing in the juices and moisture. Meat will smoke quite a bit when searing, but that means you're doing it right. Searing gives your meat a very good flavor and keeps it moist and tender on inside.

Wild Rice

2 onions, chopped
½ celery stalk, chopped
finely
1 lb. butter
1 lb. bacon, cooked very
crisp and crumbled
1 lb. wild rice (boiled
until it's curled)
salt and pepper to taste

Russell L'Allier

Saute onion and celery in butter until transparent. Mix bacon and rice together. Add butter mixture to rice and add salt and pepper to taste.

Serves: 4

Russell L'Allier
New Richmond, Wisconsin

Craig's Camp Chili

2 lbs. moose burger
1 lb. chopped moose steak
8 tsp. chili powder
2 tsp. salt
4 tsp. minced garlic

30 oz. tomato sauce
30 oz. red kidney beans
½ cup chopped onions (optional)
½ cup chopped green pepper

Brown meats in a frying pan and mix remaining ingredients in medium pot. Drain fat from meat and add to pot. Bring to a boil and cook for 5-10 minutes. Reduce heat and simmer for about ½ hour.

Serves: 8-10

Craig S. Elliott
Windham, Maine

Barbecued Elk Ribs

6 lbs. elk ribs
2-3 lbs. pork ribs
2 cups water

Cut ribs to preferable length, 3-4 ribs per section. Place in large roaster with 2 cups of water. Roast in oven at 350-400 degrees for 1 hour. Add more water if required.

Combine sauce ingredients and pour over ribs. Reduce heat and cook until tender, turning ribs occasionally.

2 cups ketchup
2 T. vinegar
2 T. lemon juice
½ cup red wine
1 pkg. dried onion soup mix
3 garlic cloves, chopped

½ tsp. salt
2 T. Worcestershire sauce
3 T. brown sugar
⅛ tsp. pepper
1 T. dry mustard

When ribs are done, cook on hot grill or over an open fire for a few minutes.

Serves: A bunch

Martin C. Carver
Surrey, British Columbia

Porcupine Meatballs

2 lbs. ground moose or elk
1 large yellow onion, chopped
1 clove garlic, chopped
2 cups cooked white rice

salt and pepper to taste
2 cans soup, tomato or
   cream of mushroom
1 soup can of milk

In a large bowl, combine ground meat, onion, garlic, rice, salt and pepper. Mix all ingredients thoroughly with hands. Make into meatballs about the size of golf balls.

Spray large baking dish (9" x 13") with non-stick oil and place meatballs in pan so they touch each other. Mix soup and milk together and pour over top. Bake at 350 degrees for 45 minutes or until done.

Serves: 6-8

Frank Albert
Manteca, California

Pickled Heart

1 big game animal heart
1 bay leaf
3 tsp. salt
1 medium onion, sliced

1 T. pickling spice
1 tsp. sugar
   white vinegar

Rinse heart and trim off excess fat. Soak overnight in salt water.

Cover heart with water, add bay leaf and salt. Cook until tender. Retain cooking water, skim off fat.

Slice heart into finger food size pieces, trimming off fat and gristle. Place heart back in pot with onion, pickling spice and sugar. Cover mixture with equal parts of retained cooking juice and white vinegar. Bring to rolling boil and cook for 1 minute.

Allow to cool and transfer all to a tight sealing jar. Best after storing in refrigerator for several weeks. May be kept in refrigerator for up to 2 years at least. Usually disappears in 10 minutes or less at card games and deer camps.

Serves: 4

Baird R. Booth
Dundee, New York

Mike Randall

Marinated Caribou Strips

1½ lbs. caribou round steak, cut
    into 11 x ¾" strips
1 cup water
1 bay leaf, broken into pieces
2 garlic cloves, minced
1 small onion, sliced

½ tsp. thyme
5 whole cloves
1 cup dry red wine
2 T. cooking oil
3 T. butter
    salt and pepper to taste

Heat water to a boil. Place bay leaf, garlic, onion, thyme and cloves in a non-metal bowl and add the boiling water. Let cool, add wine and oil, stir. Add meat to mixture. If necessary, add enough additional water to cover the meat. Cover the bowl and refrigerate for at least 2 hours.

Remove meat from the marinade and pat dry with paper towels. Heat butter in a frying pan over high heat. Add meat and fry quickly for 2-3 minutes on each side. Serve with salt and pepper.

Serves: 4

Mike Randall
Florence, Oregon

Bullwinkle Taco Salad

1 lb. moose burger (chopped up)
  or steaks sliced into thin strips
1 head lettuce, chopped
¼ cup sliced green pepper
¼ cup chopped onions
2 large or 3 small tomatoes, diced

1 8-oz. shredded cheddar cheese
¼ cup drained kidney beans
  (optional)
½ cup sliced black olives (optional)
16 oz. French or
  Catalina dressing

Brown meat and set aside to cool. Mix lettuce, green pepper, onion, tomatoes and cheese together. Add kidney beans and black olives if desired. Pour dressing in and mix well. Refrigerate for 2 hours.

Serve on salad plates or in flour tortilla bowls. Top with round taco chips.

Serves: 4

David Lawson
Townsend, Delaware

David Lawson

Newfoundland Moose Pie

1 quart jar stewed moose meat
½ onion, diced or onion powder
    to taste
½ tsp. garlic powder

1 T. salt
½ T. pepper
cornstarch to thicken
2 pie crusts (9 inches in diameter)

In a sauce pan, heat the stewed meat with all of the liquid. Add the other ingredients. When it comes to a boil, add enough cornstarch and water mixture to thicken sauce. A thicker sauce gives better results with the bottom crust.

Prick bottom of 9" pie crust with fork. Pour thickened mixture into pie crust and flatten out second pie crust to place on top of pie. Pinch edges to seal crusts and cut four 1" slits in top crust. Bake at 400 degrees for approximately 20 minutes or until top crust is browned. For an added touch, cut out a moose figure from leftover pie crust dough and place it on the center of the pie before baking.

Serves: 4-6

Steve McDyer
Kodiak, Alaska

Javelina Mexicali

2-3 lbs. javelina meat, cubed
1 onion, chopped
5 garlic cloves, sliced
1 stalk celery, sliced
1 tomato, diced
3 whole, dried red chili
    peppers, crushed

¾ cup vinegar
⅓ cup vegetable oil
1 T. seasoned salt
½ tsp. thyme
½ tsp. black ground pepper

Fill 3½ quart Crockpot ⅓ full of water. Add javelina meat and remaining ingredients, stirring thoroughly. Fill Crockpot with water to within ½" from top. Cook on low for approximately 12 hours.

Serve over tortillas or rice.

Serves: 8

Ken Hunt
Oracle, Arizona

112

Marinated Grilled Moose Steaks

4 moose steaks, ½ to 1 inch thick

For marinade, mix together:

⅓ cup Italian salad dressing
⅔ cup dry burgundy wine
    lemon pepper
3 T. Worcestershire sauce
3 T. Teriyaki

1 medium onion, chopped
1 T. garlic, minced
½ tsp. dried ginger

Place steaks in large resealable bag and pour marinade over meat. Seal and place in refrigerator for 4 hours.

Remove meat, drain and grill over hot coals until medium rare. Use marinade to baste meat while cooking.

Serves: 4

Mary Ann Keller
Parsons, Kansas

Cajun Antelope Steaks

1 lb. antelope steak, trimmed,
    in bitesize pieces
1½ T. olive oil
1 T. Cajun seasoning
½ tsp. ground red pepper
1 can stewed tomatoes
    (or Cajun style)

½ medium onion, chopped
2-3 cloves garlic, chopped
    salt
    pepper
¼ cup dry red wine
2 cups cooked rice

In a dutch oven, sear steak meat in olive oil until browned. Add remaining ingredients (except rice). Bring to a boil, then reduce heat and simmer for 1½ hours or until meat is done.

Serve over rice.

Serves: 4

Mary Ann Keller
Parsons, Kansas

Chuck Drerup

Sheep and Cabbage

5 lb. sheep brisket
2 large onions, chopped
5 large potatoes, whole
5 carrots, quartered
1 clove garlic, chopped

1 T. pepper
1 tsp. paprika
2 heads cabbage, quartered
1 T. salt

Boil brisket in covered pan on low heat for 2 hours. Add all ingredients, except cabbage and salt, and cook on low heat for 1 hour.

In another pot, cover cabbage with 1 quart of water, add salt and cook for 20 minutes over medium heat.

Slice meat and serve with cabbage and other vegetables. It will melt in your mouth!

Serves: 10-12

Chuck and Christy Drerup
Kendallville, Indiana

Shoulder Roast "Exotic Sheep"

2 lbs. sheep shoulder roast
2 cloves garlic, slivered
1 T. flour
6 large carrots

2 cups water
1 envelope dried onion soup mix
   small cooking bag

Cut up garlic and insert in meat. Put flour in cooking bag and shake to coat. Put meat and carrots in bag. Mix water with onion soup and pour over meat and carrots. Bake for 1¼ hours at 325 degrees. Make gravy out of juice from meat and carrots.

Serves: 4

Lester & Leslie Lester
Bellevue, Texas

Bear Dumpling Stew

1½ lbs. bear stew meat
1 cup celery, chopped
4 slices raw bacon
4 T. ketchup

1 onion, quartered
2 potatoes, cut into chunks
2 carrots, sliced
   salt and pepper

Brown meat in skillet. Add meat, celery, bacon, ketchup and onion to Dutch oven or slow cooker. Cover with water and cook until tender. Add potatoes and carrots. Season to taste. Cook for 2 hours in Dutch oven or in slow cooker for 2 hours on high or 6 hours on low.

Dumplings

¾ cup milk
1½ cup flour

3 tsp. baking powder
¼ tsp. salt

When you have 15 minutes left on stew, prepare dumpling mix. Stir ingredients together just until all ingredients are moistened (do not over-mix). Drop mixture onto top of stew with a tablespoon, cover pot and keep lid on for 12 minutes. Can be prepared over a campfire.

Serves: 4-6

Susan VanKekerix
Two Harbors, Minnesota

Stir Frying is for the Bears

1 lb. bear meat, cut into bitesized pieces	1 tsp. cornstarch
1 tsp. soy sauce	1 tsp. salt
1 T. oil	pinch pepper

Mix all ingredients together, except bear meat, to make marinade. Pour over meat and let marinate for 1 hour or longer, stirring every 15 minutes.

2 T. oil	3-4 cloves garlic, chopped
1 large onion, diced	6-8 fresh mushrooms

Set fry pan or wok on medium to high setting. Add oil and spread over bottom of pan. Add onion and garlic and stir fry for one minute. Add mushrooms and saute until slightly tender, about 2 minutes. Take this mixture out of the pan and put in a bowl.

Saute bear in same pan (bear meat needs to be well done). When done, take the meat out of the pan and put in the bowl with the onion mixture.

fresh vegetables of your choice	3 T. water
1 can chicken broth	1 tsp. sugar
1 T. soy sauce	2 T. Green onion, chopped
1 T. corn starch	cooked rice

Clean fresh vegetables and cut into bitesized pieces (your choice of green pepper, red pepper, broccoli, cauliflower, celery, carrots). Saute vegetables in same pan for 3-4 minutes. Stir in chicken broth and soy sauce. Add meat and onion mixture. Heat until broth begins to steam.

Mix together cornstarch, water and sugar. Add to the meat and vegetables and stir until thickened lightly.

Serve with rice and garnish with chopped green onion.

Serves: 4

Tom Hackler
Corcoran, Minnesota

Tom Hackler

Slow Cooked Bear Stew

2 lbs. bear meat, cubed
½ cup flour
1 tsp. paprika
¼ tsp. pepper
1 tsp. salt
2 cloves garlic, crushed
2 stalks celery, chopped

2 cups carrot chunks
1 large onion, chopped
1½ cups mushrooms
4 medium potatoes, cubed
2 cups beef broth
2 T. soy sauce
2 T. Worcestershire sauce

Place flour, paprika, pepper, salt, garlic and bear meat in slow coooker. Toss to coat with flour. Add vegetables and mix. Combine broth, soy sauce and Worcestershire sauce and pour into pot. Cook on low for 8-10 hours. Stir before serving.

Serves: 4-6

Jim and Cheryl Camenisch
Oglesby, Illinois

Roast Boar with Polish Stuffing

    1 young boar, cleaned
  2-3 onions, finely chopped
    3 T. lard
    2 cups bread crumbs
    1 cup milk
    1 boar heart, ground
    1 boar liver, ground
  ½ cup butter
    3 egg yolks
    3 egg whites, stiffly beaten
      salt and pepper to taste
    1 tsp. marjoram
    1 tsp. nutmeg
    3 T. chopped fresh parsley

Salt boar well and let stand 1 hour.

Saute onions in lard until golden. Soak bread crumbs in milk. Cream butter with egg yolks. Combine ingredients, fold in egg whites and season with salt, pepper, marjoram, nutmeg and parsley.

Fill baby boar with mixture and sew it up. Increase or decrease the amount of stuffing depending on the size of your boar. Roast on rack in pan, uncovered, at 350 degrees, brushing often with the pan drippings or melted butter. Roasting time will depend on the size of the boar. It is done when fork tender and when juice that oozes out is no longer pink.

Serves: A group

Andrew Nowinski
Mt. Prospect, Illinois

Grilled Antelope

1-2 lbs. antelope meat, cut into 1½" cubes
½ cup melted margarine or butter
½ cup soy sauce

Dip meat cubes in blend of margarine and soy sauce. Cook over medium heat on grill, basting frequently with butter and soy sauce mixture until medium done (slightly pink inside). Serve while hot and enjoy.

Serves: 4-6

James Price
Micanopy, Florida

Stuff Over Rice

1½ lb. moose, cubed
½ cup flour
1 tsp. salt
½ tsp. pepper
½ tsp. chili powder
2 T. cooking oil or fat
1 medium onion, chopped

1 cup chopped celery
  ground pepper (optional)
1 quart tomatoes
1 can kidney beans
2 or more cups prepared rice

Mix flour, salt, pepper and chili powder. Roll moose cubes in flour mixture. Brown in any type of cooking oil or fat. Remove meat from pan and set aside. Saute onion, celery and green pepper in the remaining fat. Put meat back in pan. Add tomatoes, cover and simmer for 1½ hours or until fork-tender. Stir occasionally, adding small amounts of water if meat starts sticking. Taste and add more salt, pepper or chili powder to taste. Add the kidney beans for the last 45 minutes. Serve over the rice.

Serves: 4-6

JoAnn Moskiewicz
Gilman, Wisconsin

Marinated Bear Steaks with Wine

    4 lbs. bear steaks approximately 1" thick
   10 fresh mushrooms, sliced
    2 T. butter

Remove as much fat as possible from meat and tenderize with a meat mallet.

Marinade

   2-4 cups of your favorite berry, dandelion or other sweet wine
     1 cup olive oil
     2 medium onions, diced
     3 carrots, diced
    ½ can frozen orange juice
     1 bay leaf
    ½ tsp. thyme
     1 tsp. paprika

Pat McGraw

Mix marinade ingredients together. Add tenderized steaks and marinate for 48 hours in refrigerator, turning occasionally. Remove meat from marinade.

Steaks can be cooked on grill or broiler, basting with marinade. Saute mushrooms in butter and pour over top of meat before serving.

Serves: 8

*Pat and Susan McGraw
Saginaw, Michigan*

Jim Camenisch

Bear Chops

4-6 bear chops	1 can cream of celery soup
¼ cup butter	1 pkg. dried onion soup mix
2 cloves garlic, crushed	2 T. beef soup base
1 can cream of mushroom soup	2 cups water

In skillet, brown chops in butter and remove from pan. Saute garlic in same pan 1 minute. Add soups, soup mix, soup base and water and blend until smooth. Add chops and simmer about 1½ hours or until tender.

Delicious with wild rice or egg noodles.

Serves: 4

Jim and Cheryl Camenisch
Oglesby, Illinois

Moose Meatballs

3 lbs. ground moose
1 medium potato, chopped
1 onion, grated
1 large egg

1 tsp. garlic powder
salt and pepper to taste
12 oz. ketchup
1 liter ginger ale

Place ground moose in a large bowl. Add potato, onion, egg, garlic powder, salt and pepper. Mix well. Roll into small balls and brown in an oiled frying pan, then place in Crockpot. Pour ketchup and ginger ale over meatballs and mix well. Cook on low setting for 4-5 hours.

Serves: 12

Allen Bluhm
Lake Ann, Michigan

Barbecued Antelope

1½ lbs. antelope backstraps
1 cup flour
1 T. pepper

1 T. all season salt
5 T. cooking oil

Mix dry ingredients together in bowl. Coat meat with flour mixture and fry in pan with hot oil until brown on both sides. Remove from heat. Put into Crockpot or slow cooker.

Mix the following sauce ingredients together:

1 cup vinegar
1 cup prepared mustard
1 cup molasses
¼ cup ketchup
2 tsp. Worcestershire sauce

Mix well and pour over meat. Set Crockpot on low for 7-8 hours. Goes good with baked potatoes or potato salad.

Serves: 4

Michael Van Dyke
Antler, North Dakota

Moose Tongue

1 moose tongue
2 garlic cloves, minced
1 small onion, chopped
¼ tsp. Worcestershire sauce
¼ tsp. soy sauce
⅛ tsp. black pepper
2 bay leaves

BIG GAME

Cover tongue with water and other ingredients and boil 3-4 hours, adding water as required. When fully cooked, allow to cool and peel off outer layer of tongue. Slice thin and dip in hot mustard or use in sandwiches.

Serves: 2-4

Martin C. Carver
Surrey, British Columbia

Moose Nose

1 moose nose
1 large onion, sliced

Cut off the large upper jaw of a moose just below the eyes.

Simmer in a pot of boiling water for an hour, cool and pull out the loosened hairs. Wash clean.

Return to a cleaned pot. Cover with fresh water, add salt and onion. Cook just short of boiling until the dark meat falls away from the bones and jowls and white stripes ease from the nostrils. If the sweet tantalizing odors have been too much for you, this is fine to pick at hot. If you can keep occupied with different tidbits, however, alternate bites of both kinds of meat in a small narrow pan. Strain the liquid over them, let the juices and the meat jell together overnight and savor the whole in cold slices.

Serves: 4

R. L. Johnson
Anaconda, Montana

Dwight Clark

Wild Boar Sloppy Joes

2 lbs. wild boar meat, ground
2 stalks celery, sliced
1 large onion, diced
2 cups ketchup

Brown meat in skillet for 30 minutes on low. Stir in celery, onion and ketchup. Simmer for 30-45 minutes.

Serve on hamburger buns or open-faced on Texas toast.

Serves: 8

Dwight Clark
Columbus, Ohio

Spiced Skewered Boar

It may be tempting to forgo marinating the boar, especially as every kitchen may not have all the necessary spices. Don't do it. By the way, use fresh spices whenever possible. If you have to use spices you've had around for awhile, increase the portions listed below.

This is a modification of a Spanish tapas (with, I suspect, a strong Moorish tradition) and is unique - not too hot, not too spicy. I find that is especially good if grilled over an intense charcoal fire; but, I have enjoyed it broiled in the oven.

BIG GAME

1 lb. boneless boar loin, cut in 1" cubes
1-2 cloves garlic, minced or crushed
1 tsp. ground cumin
¼ T. ground coriander

1 tsp. paprika
¼ tsp. crushed red pepper
2 T. olive oil
freshly ground black pepper

Mix everything except the boar in a non-metallic bowl (you don't want to give this a "tinny" taste). Add boar and stir until it is evenly coated with the marinade. Cover and refrigerate at least a couple of hours (overnight is even better).

Put boar on skewers. Grill over a hot charcoal fire (or broil about 4" from flame) turning once. You don't want to undercook the boar, so I suggest about 4 min. total cooking time.

Serves: 4

Keith Baker
Falls Church, Virginia

Boar Meatloaf

¾ lb. ground boar
¾ lb. ground beef
1 egg
½ cup milk
¾ cup Italian bread crumbs
¼ cup chopped onion
1 tsp. salt

1 pinch pepper
½ cup ketchup or barbecue sauce
¼ cup chopped green peppers
¼ cup chopped celery
1 4-oz. can mushrooms pieces and
    stems, drained

Lightly coat meatloaf pan with ketchup. Mix all other ingredients together including remaining ketchup. Mold into pan and cook 1¼ - 1½ hours at 375 degrees.

Serves: 4-6

Bob Trenholm
Easton, Massachusetts

Game and Tongue Soup

1 lb. bones or stew meat	1 rounded tsp. pepper
1 tongue from deer, elk, etc.	1 tsp. dried garlic
4 beef bouillon cubes	1½ cups rice
2 bay leaves	1 pkg. mixed frozen vegetables
1 tsp. dry basil	water
1 tsp. Beau Monde	

In a pressure cooker, combine bones, meat and spices. Add water to cover and cook for 45 minutes. After the pressure goes down, remove lid. Remove the meat, bones and bay leaves. Set aside. To the remaining broth, add the rice and vegetables and bring to a boil. Reduce heat to a simmer, stirring as needed to prevent sticking. Remove meat from the bones, cut off excess fat. Also remove skin from the tongue and cut meat into pieces. Add all of the meat back into the soup and allow to simmer until the rice is tender and has absorbed most of the liquid.

Serves: 8

John Rickelman
St. Anthony, Indiana

Grilled Antelope Steaks

4 antelope steaks
1 cup Italian salad
     dressing

Thaw steaks, pour Italian salad dressing over steaks and marinate overnight in a covered glass dish or in a resealable plastic bag. Remove meat and drain. Grill on barbecue pit until slightly pink inside.

Serves: 4

Tally Stone
Puyallup, Washington

Tally Stone

126

Sheep Soup

3 lbs. sheep, cut into ½" cubes
3 quarts water
3 T. butter
1 clove garlic, chopped
1 T. onion salt
2 large onions, chopped

2 large onions, chopped
1 T. dried dill
½ cup parsley flakes
1 8-oz. can water chestnuts
1 lb. fresh mushrooms,
    sliced

Boil sheep meat about 15 minutes and skim residue off surface. When water is clear, add remaining ingredients and stir. Cook on low heat for about 1½ hours, stirring occasionally. Enjoy this rare favorite!

Serves: 8

Chuck and Christy Drerup
Kendallville, Indiana

Alligator Italian Style

4 T. extra virgin olive oil
3 cloves, minced
1 12-oz. can crushed or cubed
    Italian style tomatoes
¼ cup chopped black olives
1 T. capers, rinsed
1 tsp. cayenne pepper

½ tsp. oregano
2 oz. flat anchovies, chopped
1 T. dried parsley
¾ lb. scallops
¾ lb. alligator tail, cubed and boiled
1½ lbs. spaghetti noodles
¼ stick butter

Add first 9 ingredients to Dutch oven and heat over medium temperature for about 20 minutes. At the same time, cook noodles until done and drain, add butter and mix well to coat. Add scallops (which cook fast) and alligator tail to Dutch oven. Cook at medium for 5 minutes more.

Serve over noodles with garlic bread, Parmesan cheese and plenty of cold beer.

Serves: 4-6

Jack D. Hunter, II
Harlingen, Texas

Goat Sauerbraten

3-4 lb. goat roast
  salt and cracked black pepper

Marinade

1⁄2 pint water and 1 cup strong
    black coffee
1 pint wine vinegar or dry red wine
1 onion, chopped
3 cloves garlic, crushed
2 bay leaves
6 peppercorns, bruised

5 cloves
2 T. flour
2 T. bacon fat
2 T. brown sugar
6 crushed gingersnaps

Rinse roast, wipe dry, rub all over with salt and pepper. Set in large glass or plastic container.

Add marinade ingredients to a pot, mix well and bring to a boil. cooking for 5-10 minutes. Let cool, then pour over meat and place in refrigerator for 24 - 48 hours, turning meat occasionally.

To cook, heat Dutch oven with drippings or fat while draining meat and coating with flour. Brown meat on all sides being careful not to penetrate meat with fork while turning. When brown, add 2 cups marinade, cover tightly and simmer 2½ hours.

Remove meat, add sugar and crushed gingersnaps to liquid in pan. Return to quick boil for 2 minutes. If gravy is not as thick as you like, add mixture of 1 tsp. cornstarch to ¼ cup water to thicken.

Serves: 8-12

Burke's Ranch
Cottonwood, California

Small Game

Porcupine
Rabbit
Turtle

Raccoon
Armadillo
Squirrel
Woodchuck

Kevin's Rabbit Stew

2 rabbits
6 potatoes
4 carrots, chopped
1 shot of brandy
½ tsp. pepper
28 oz. mushroom gravy

Field dress and clean the rabbits. Soak them in cold salt water for about 8 to 10 hours to remove any blood shot. Cut each rabbit into 2-4 pieces then put into a slow cooker or crock-pot. Peal potatoes and add with carrots into the cooker. Add brandy, pepper and cook for 3-4 hours. Drain cooker and pour mushroom gravy, heated, over the rabbit chunks, potatoes and carrots.

Kevin White

Serves: 6-8

Kevin White
Oshkosh, Wisconsin

Grandpa's Snapper Soup

1 large turtle
6 boiled eggs, sliced
½ tsp. celery seed

1 stick butter
lima beans, carrots, celery, onion
chopped, potatoes, chopped

Hang turtle upside down for 1 hour after cutting head off. Dip in boiling water, and peel scales off (dip again if needed). Scrap bottom of turtle and pull toe nails off. Cut around breast bone to remove intestines.

In a large pot, soak turtle in salt water for 1-2 hours before cooking. Bring water to boil and cook until shell falls off, remove shell from water. Add eggs, celery seed, butter and vegetables to broth. Use 1 quart of each vegetable for a 5-7 pound turtle. You may use a little more or less depending on your taste.

Serves: a large group

Melissa G. Darnell
Ronda, North Carolina

Southern Fried Armadillo (Texas Style)

1 armadillo, quartered and
    deboned
½ tsp. salt
¼ tsp. pepper

⅛ tsp. red pepper (optional)
flour
cooking oil

Cut meat into small steaks. Mix salt and peppers together and sprinkle both sides of steaks. Coat both sides of meat with flour. Fry meat in preheated cooking oil over medium heat until both sides are brown. When both sides are golden brown, meat is done. Armadillo meat is very tender.

Serves: 4

Neil Means
Spurger, Texas

Turtle Soup

1⅓ lbs. turtle meat
4½ cups water
2 medium onions
1 bay leaf
¼ tsp. cayenne pepper
1¼ tsp. salt
¼ cup lemon juice
5 T. butter

3 T. Worcestershire sauce
⅓ cup flour
2 hard boiled eggs, sliced
3 T. tomato puree
⅓ cup chicken broth fresh
    parsley, chopped

Bring turtle meat and water to boil and skim off the foam. Chop 1 onion and set aside. Quarter the other onion and add to pot with bay leaf, cayenne pepper and salt. Cover and simmer for 2 hours or until meat is tender. Remove meat and cut into ½" cubes and set aside. Strain broth and set aside.

Melt butter in sauce pan, add chopped onion and cook until tender. Add flour, stirring until lightly browned. Whisk in reserved broth. Cook and stir until thickened. Reduce heat, add tomato puree and Worcestershire sauce. Simmer, uncovered for 10 minutes. Add chicken broth, eggs, lemon juice and meat. Simmer until heated through. Garnish with parsley.

Serves: 8-12

Scott Thompson
Greeley, Colorado

Barbecue Raccoon

1 medium or large raccoon
1 T. salt

Clean raccoon. Clean away any visible fat. Cut into pieces. Place into pressure cooker. Cover half way with water. Add salt. Cook at 10 pounds pressure for about 1 hour. If raccoon is falling off bone, it is ready. Remove meat from bone. Remove any trace of fat at all. Place clean, cooked meat into heavy pot so you can simmer it with the sauce.

Sauce

1 8-oz. can tomato sauce
½ cup chopped onion
¼ cup chopped green pepper
1 T. brown sugar
1 T. vinegar

1 T. Worcestershire sauce
1 T. prepared mustard
1 tsp. chili powder
1 clove garlic, minced

Mix all ingredients in a sauce pan and bring to a slow simmer. Simmer for 15 minutes. Pour sauce over meat in heavy pot. Simmer on low heat for 1 hour or longer if wanted.

Serves: 6-8

Daniel E. Franks
Fruita, Colorado

Baked Coon and Onion

1 medium or large raccoon
1 pkg. dried onion soup mix
2 large onions, sliced

1 can tomatoes, chopped
salt and pepper to taste

Cut raccoon in pieces. Clean out scent glands and fat. Place raccoon in pot and cover with water. Add salt and pepper and cook until half cooked. Remove raccoon, drain and save stock. Place raccoon in roasting pan and pour stock in pan until half of the raccoon is covered. Sprinkle raccoon with onion soup mix, salt and pepper, onions and tomatoes. Cover and cook at 325 degrees until done. Baste a couple of times while cooking.

Serves: 6-8

Richard Gayewski
Webster, Massachusetts

Turkey's Baked Groundhog

1 dressed groundhog
3-4 strips of bacon
1 bag seasoned dressing
salt and pepper to taste

Stuff groundhog with dressing. Put belly down on baking dish. Put bacon strips over the back of groundhog, and any extra dressing along the sides. Cover with foil and bake at 350 degrees for 1½ hours or until tender.

Serves: 2

Ronald Brindle
Kenosha, Wisconsin

Rabbit with Gingersnaps

2-3 rabbits, cut into bitesized pieces
2 lbs. gingersnaps
2 eggs
1 large onion, chopped
8 slices bacon (family secret for keeping meat moist)
cooking oil

Crush gingersnaps to make breading. Set aside. Mix eggs with a little water in a bowl. In a large skillet, pour enough oil to go up sides of pan about ½". Heat oil on medium high heat, add some onion. Dip rabbit in eggs, then in gingersnaps. Fry to golden brown on all sides. Put in roasting pan until all the rabbit is browned. Add remaining onion and more oil as needed.

When all the rabbit is browned, put bacon over top. Cover with foil and bake at 325 degrees for 1-1½ hours, until tender and moist. Remove foil for last 15 minutes to let crust get crisp.

Serves: 8

Kathy Artman
Atlanta, Michigan

Squirrel Skillet Pie

1 squirrel, cleaned and cut up
½ tsp. salt
½ cup chopped celery
½ cup margarine
¼ cup minced onion
¼ cup sweet red or green pepper, chopped
¼ cup flour
2 cans ready-to-bake biscuits
salt and pepper

Cover squirrel pieces with water and add salt. Add chopped celery, cover and simmer until meat is tender. Remove meat, but save cooking liquid. Cool meat and pull from bones. Set aside.

In large iron skillet, melt margarine over low heat. Add onion and peppers and cook about 5 minutes, until onion is transparent. Blend in flour and cook until mixture bubbles, stirring constantly. Pour in 2 cups cooking liquid. Cook until thick and smooth, stirring constantly. Season with salt and pepper. Add meat and reheat to boiling. Top with canned biscuits and bake at 350 degrees for 10-12 minutes until biscuits are brown.

Serves: 4-6

Clara Sawlaw
Paris, Illinois

Mexican Rabbit

1 rabbit
1 can chili beans
1 pkg. taco seasoning
½ tsp. cayenne pepper
1 pkg. Spanish rice
1 16-oz. pkg. taco seasoned cheese
16 oz. sour cream
tortilla chips or taco shells

Parboil meat until ready to come off the bone. Let cool. Remove meat from bone. Mix meat with beans in pan. Add taco seasoning, cayenne pepper and enough water to keep ingredients from burning. Let simmer for ½ hour.

Put box of Spanish rice in casserole dish. Add 1 cup water and meat, stirring together. Add layer of cheese over top. Bake at 275 degrees for 45-60 minutes. Remove from oven and add layer of sour cream, another layer of cheese, a layer of tortilla chips or broken taco shells, and another layer of cheese. Bake until cheese is melted.

Serves: 4

Mark Carmack
Rives Junction, Michigan

Cream Soup Rabbit

2 medium to large rabbits, cleaned
1 large onion, chopped
1 can cream of celery soup
1 can cream of chicken soup
black pepper

Place rabbits on their backs in a large baking pan. Sprinkle with black pepper. Place onion in the rabbits stomach cavities.

Mix soups together in a bowl undiluted then pour over rabbits, making sure to cover them with soup. Bake at 350 degrees for 1 hour, with the pan covered for the first 30 minutes, then uncovered for the last 30 minutes.

Serves: 6-8

James E. Robertson
Rutledge, Missouri

Rabbit Dijon

2 rabbits, cleaned, deboned and cut into serving pieces
4 T. butter or olive oil
2 cloves garlic, minced
2 cups half and half
4 T. Dijon mustard
1 tsp. onion powder
½ tsp. white pepper
½ tsp. salt
¼ tsp. cayenne pepper
flour

Soak rabbit meat in salted water for 1-2 hours. Drain and thoroughly rinse in fresh water. Melt 2 tablespoons butter or olive oil in a skillet or fry pan. Dust the meat with flour and cook until well browned on both sides. Remove the meat to a plate.

Melt the rest of the butter in the pan. Add the minced garlic and stir. After about 2 minutes, add 2 tablespoons flour and stir into a thick paste. Using a whisk, stir in the half and half. This will thicken into a gravy. Add the remaining ingredients and keep stirring until well mixed and the sauce has a nice, thick consistency.

Put the rabbit pieces back into the pan with the Dijon sauce. Simmer for about 20 minutes. Serve the rabbit on a platter and spoon sauce over the top.

Serves: 6-8

Ron North
San Clemente, California

Baked Rabbit Italiano

2 rabbit hindquarters, halved
2 rabbit loins
1 jar mushroom spaghetti sauce
1 T. minced garlic
½ tsp. oregano
½ tsp. basil
¼ tsp. creole seasoning
1 4-oz. can mushroom pieces and stems, drained
¼ cup Parmesan cheese
½ lb. grated mozzarella cheese

Rinse rabbit thoroughly in cold water; set aside. In a 9" x 12" baking pan, mix together spaghetti sauce, seasonings, mushrooms and Parmesan cheese. Arrange rabbit pieces on top of sauce. Seal pan tightly with foil. Bake at 350 degrees for 1¼ hours.

Remove foil from pan and top rabbit pieces with mozzarella cheese. Return pan to oven and bake an additional 15 minutes or until cheese is melted and bubbly. Serve over hot angel hair pasta with a salad and toasted garlic bread.

Serves: 6-8

William Soltis
Saginaw, Michigan

Dijon and Wine Rabbit

1 large rabbit, cut into serving sized pieces
2 T. olive oil
2 yellow onions, thinly sliced
2-3 garlic cloves, minced
½ tsp. dried rosemary
½ tsp. dried sage
½ tsp. dried oregano
1½ cups white wine
2 chopped leeks (white and light green part only)
1½ T. Dijon mustard
½ cup half and half
salt and pepper to taste

Brown rabbit over medium high heat in olive oil. Saute onion and garlic in separate pan and add to rabbit. Reduce heat to low, add herbs and white wine. Cover and simmer 45 minutes.

Add chopped leeks, cover and cook down, approximately 5-10 minutes. Remove rabbit to serving dish, leaving onion mixture in pan. Add remaining ingredients and simmer to reduce liquid, about 5-10 minutes. Pour sauce over rabbit and serve.

Serves: 3-4

Diane Sandoval
Issaquah, Washingto

136

Fried Squirrel

- 1 squirrel, cleaned and quartered
- 1 small onion, chopped
- 2 stalks celery, chopped
   salt and pepper to taste

Place squirrel in pan and cover with water. Add onion and celery and season to taste. Boil squirrel for about 20 minutes. Remove from pan, rinse and let cool.

Batter

- 1 cup flour
- 1 egg
- ½ cup milk
   salt and pepper to taste

Mix all ingredients together until you have a smooth batter. Place squirrel sections in batter and deep fry until golden brown.

Serves: 2

Bud Stillwagon
Dover, New Hampshire

Rocky Stew

- 1 raccoon, cleaned
- 4 carrots, chopped
- 3 potatoes, chopped
- 2 stalks celery, chopped
- 1 bag frozen mixed vegetables
   your favorite stew seasonings

Remove glands and as much fat as you can from raccoon. Parboil until done, skimming fat off water as it rises to the top. Remove raccoon and let cool. Debone meat and hold aside.

Add carrots, potatoes and mixed vegetables. Return meat to the pot. Add seasonings. Keep at a low simmer until ready to serve. For thicker stew, add flour mixed with cold water before serving, stir until thickened.

Serves: 4

Gordon Bender
DeWitt, Iowa

Raccoon Patties

4 cups ground raccoon meat
1 cup bread crumbs
1 tsp. salt
¼ tsp. pepper
½ tsp. ground sage
1 beaten egg
½ cup chopped onion

Mix all ingredients together well. Make into patties and fry in small amount of light oil. Great for breakfast or on burger buns.

Serves: 6-8

Gordon Bender
DeWitt, Iowa

Saucy Gameburger

cooking oil
1 lb. ground game meat
2 T. flour
½ cup milk
½ cup onion, minced
salt and pepper to taste

Put a little cooking oil into a heavy skillet. Crumble gameburger into the oil and stir over medium heat until evenly browned. Add flour and continue to stir until thickened. You may need to adjust the amount of flour used — it will depend on how much fat is in the pan after meat has browned.

Add milk and stir until it bubbles and thickens. Add minced onion, salt and pepper to taste.

Serve over rice or noodles.

Serves: 4

Donald Strom
Anacortes, Washington

Game Birds

Dove
Grouse
Partridge

Pheasants
Quail
Turkey

Batter Fried Partridge

4 partridge breasts
  pancake flour
1 can beer
3 cups soda cracker crumbs, seasoned to taste
  cooking oil

Bone partridge breasts and cut into serving sized pieces. Dip pieces of meat in pancake flour, then in beer and roll in soda cracker crumbs. Deep fry in hot oil until golden brown.

Serves: 2-4

Donald Witt
Tunnel City, Wisconsin

Pheasant Fricassee

2 large pheasants, cleaned
3 T. butter or margarine
1 medium onion, chopped
1½ cups celery, chopped
2 14-oz. cans chicken broth
3 extra large eggs, beaten
1 can cream of mushroom soup
1½ cups grated American or cheddar cheese
1 8-oz. box Ritz crackers, rolled into fine crumbs
½ tsp. salt
½ tsp. pepper

Place pheasants in dutch oven, cover with salted water and cook over medium heat until done. Pull meat off bones in bitesized pieces. After cooling, place broth in refrigerator and leave until fat rises to top. Remove fat from surface of broth and save 4 cups. Melt butter in dutch oven. Add onion and celery, saute until onion is transparent. Combine pheasant pieces with onion and celery mixture, add broth, eggs, soup, cheese, crackers, salt and pepper. Stir until blended. Pour mixture into a shallow casserole (9" x 13") and bake, uncovered, at 350 degrees for one hour or until bubbly.

Serves: 12

Dale Beisner
Natoma, Kansas

Talbot's Famous Pheasant

2 whole, cut-up pheasants, skinned and rinsed
1 cup flour
   salt and pepper to taste
   cooking oil
1 pint heavy cream

Combine flour, salt and pepper. Coat pheasant pieces with flour mixture. Fry in oil until lightly browned. Put in baking dish and pour cream over top of meat. Bake, covered, at 350 degrees for 1½ hours or until cream is thickened.

Serves: 8

Clair A. Talbot
Spanish Fork, Utah

Reed's Pheasant

1 pheasant, deboned and cut into strips
2 T. olive oil
1 pkg. dried onion soup mix
½ pint light cream
¼ cup sherry or white wine
1 tsp. freshly chopped parsley
   flour

Roll pheasant pieces in flour. Heat oil in skillet and lightly brown pheasant pieces. Remove from skillet and put in an ungreased baking dish. Mix remaining ingredients together and pour over meat. Bake at 325 degrees for 45 minutes. Serve with wild rice or freshly made egg noodles.

Serves: 4

Reed and Karen Christensen
Reisterstown, Maryland

Reed Christensen

Pheasant Tenders

2 pheasant breasts, boned
2 eggs
    finely crushed saltine crackers
    blue cheese dressing

Slice breasts into small strips about 2" x 2". Whip eggs in a bowl. Dip strips in egg, then in the cracker crumbs. Drop into deep fryer for about 2 minutes. Take out and let drain on paper towels. Dip strips in blue cheese and serve.

Serves: 4

C. Jay Simpson
Anita, Pennsylvania

Pheasant Goody Goody

2 pheasant breasts, boned
½ tsp. garlic salt
4 T. butter
1 large onion, chopped
1 green pepper, chopped
5-8 shots Worcestershire sauce
1 can cream of mushroom soup
    salt and pepper to taste

Season the pheasant breasts with salt, pepper and garlic salt. In a frying plan, melt butter and add onion and green pepper. Saute for approximately 5 minutes, then add meat and let fry for approximately 15-20 minutes. Stir in Worcestershire sauce and mushroom soup. Let simmer for 30-40 minutes. Can be served over rice or noodles.

Serves: 2

Dennis Rieth
Conway Springs, Kansas

Smothered Baked Pheasant

2 pheasants, cut up
1 can cream of mushroom soup
1 package dried onion soup mix
1 clove garlic, minced
½ cup sauterne

Place pheasant in baking pan. Mix all ingredients together and pour over pheasant. Bake, covered, at 350 degrees until tender, about 2 hours.

Serves: 6

Keith Shepherd
Shiloh, Ohio

Pheasant Spread

4 pheasant breast halves
2 stalks celery
1 very small onion
1 T. dill weed

1 tsp. Beau Monde
salt to taste
salad dressing
mayonnaise

Boil pheasant breasts in plain water until done (about 30-45 minutes, depending on size). Process in food processor until chopped fine. Finely chop celery and onion. Add to chopped pheasant.

Add two parts salad dressing to one part mayonnaise until spread is at smooth consistency. Add dill weed, Beau Monde and salt to taste. Mix well and refrigerate. Best if refrigerated at least 4 hours or overnight. Keeps well for 3-5 days in refrigerator.

This spread is excellent on crackers as a snack, on toast with lettuce or on a toasted onion bagel.

Serves: 4

Jim & Bev Van Geffen
Appleton, Wisconsin

Pheasant Tetrazzini

2 cups cooked pheasant, cut in small pieces
1 T. flour
1 T. butter
1¼ cup milk
¼ tsp. salt
¼ tsp. pepper
¼ tsp. paprika

1 T. lemon juice
1 cup cooked noodles (spaghetti or other fancy noodles)
½ cup chopped mushrooms
¼ tsp. minced garlic in liquid
½ cup finely chopped onion
Parmesan cheese

Cook over medium heat to make a medium white sauce of the flour, butter, milk and salt. Add pepper, paprika and lemon juice to sauce and heat to boiling. Add pheasant and cooked noodles. Saute mushrooms, garlic and onions in a small amount of butter and add to meat mixture. Fill greased casserole with the mixture and sprinkle top with Parmesan cheese and bread crumbs. Bake at 425 degrees about 15 minutes or until the crumbs are very brown and ingredients are bubbly.

Variation: Instead of sprinkling Parmesan cheese on top with the bread crumbs, shredded cheese can be used.

Serves: 4

Jim & Bev Van Geffen
Appleton, Wisconsin

Bear's Quail and Wild Rice

8 quail
2 envelopes dried onion soup mix
2 boxes Uncle Ben's Wild Rice mix

Preheat oven to 350 degrees. Mix soup according to directions using warm water. Place birds in 8½" x 11" baking dish. Pour soup over birds. Cover with foil and bake 30 minutes. Uncover, turn birds and bake another 30 minutes.

Meanwhile, prepare rice. Spread rice in serving dish. Place birds on top of rice. Sprinkle with parsley and serve.

Serves: 4

Brian Braymen
Mendota, Illinois

Pheasant with Wine Kraut

2 pheasants, cleaned and quartered
¼ cup butter or margarine
4-6 cups fresh sauerkraut
2 apples, cored and chopped
3 slices bacon, cut in half
1 cup white wine

Wash and dry pheasant pieces and saute in melted butter for approximately 15 minutes or until nicely browned. While this is cooking, drain sauerkraut, rinse with cold water and mix with apples.

Arrange pheasant pieces in a deep casserole dish and pour the remaining butter from pan over them. Surround bird pieces with the sauerkraut and apples, then arrange bacon slices over top. Pour wine over all. Cover the casserole and cook in oven at 250 degrees for about 1 hour or until pheasant is tender.

Remove bird pieces to warm platter. Arrange the kraut around the pheasant pieces and serve immediately.

Serves: 4-6

John A. Phillips
Wilmette, Illinois

Pheasant Casserole

1 pheasant
½ cup oil
1 cup flour
1 tsp. salt
¼ tsp. pepper
1 can cream of mushroom soup plus 1 can milk
1 small onion, finely chopped

Cut pheasant in serving sized pieces. Mix flour, salt and pepper. Dip pheasant pieces in flour mixture and fry in oil until golden brown. Place meat in a 2 quart casserole dish. Add drippings from skillet, mushroom soup, milk and onion. Bake in a 325 degree oven for 2 hours.

Serves: 3-4

Michael Long
Longmont, Colorado

Deep Fried Pheasant with Dunking Sauce

2 large pheasants, cut into peices
2 tsp. salt
¾ cup flour
¼ cup cornstarch
1 tsp. baking powder
½ tsp. salt
½ tsp. nutmeg
2 eggs
½ cup beer or milk
oil for deep frying
water

In large pot, cover pheasant pieces with water. Add salt and bring to a boil. Simmer, covered until almost tender, about 30 minutes. Remove from broth and cool.

To make batter, mix flour, cornstarch, baking powder, salt and nutmeg. Combine eggs and beer or milk and add gradually to dry ingredients, mixing to a smooth paste. Dip pheasant pieces in batter and deep fry in oil at 375 degrees until golden brown, about 10 minutes. Serve with dunking sauce.

Dunking Sauce

1 7¼-oz. can tomato sauce
½ cup sweet pickle relish, drained
1 T. prepared mustard
1 T. molasses
dash tabasco sauce

Combine all ingredients. Heat just to boiling. Serve in small individual dishes with pheasant. Makes about 1½ cups.

Serves: 4-6

Duane Wolfgang
Williamstown, Pennsylvania

Pheasant Supreme

- 1 pheasant breast
- 1 egg, beaten
- 1 20-oz. can pineapple chunks
- ⅓ cup sugar
- 2 T. cornstarch
- 4 drops yellow food coloring
  - fine cracker crumbs

Cut pheasant into bitesized pieces and season to taste. Roll in beaten egg, then in cracker crumbs. Brown on all sides in deep fat. For an oriental flavor, cook pineapple, sugar, cornstarch and food coloring until thickened. Pour over pheasant and serve immediately.

Serves: 2

Michael Long
Longmont, Colorado

Pheasant Jambalaya

- 2 large pheasants, cleaned
  - water
- 3 tsp. salt
- ¼ tsp. pepper
- 1 bay leaf
- 1 large onion, chopped (2 cups)
- 1 large clove garlic, crushed
- 1 lb. cooked ham, cubed
- 1 large can tomatoes
- 1 large green pepper, chopped
- ½ tsp. thyme, crumbled
- ¼ tsp. cayenne
- 1 cup uncooked regular rice

Put pheasants in a Dutch oven and cover with water. Add salt, pepper and bay leaf. Cook until done. Cool and remove meat from bones. Cut into cubes and set aside.

Pour broth into measuring bowl and add water to make 2 cups if necessary. Remove bay leaf. Set aside.

Saute onion and garlic in water. Add ham, tomatoes, green pepper, thyme, cayenne, pheasants and broth. Heat to boiling. Stir in rice and cook on low heat until done.

Serves: 8

Bill Gross
Oberlin, Kansas

Grouse with Lime

6 grouse breast halves
1 fresh lime
½ cup flour
1 tsp. salt
⅛ tsp. pepper

1 T. vegetable oil
2 T. brown sugar
½ cup chicken broth
½ cup white wine

Wash grouse and pat dry. Peel lime, grate peel and set aside. Squeeze juice from lime and pour over grouse. Put flour, salt and pepper in resealable plastic bag. Place breast halves in bag and shake until covered.

Heat vegetable oil in non-stick skillet. Brown breast halves on both sides. Place in a baking dish. Combine lime peel and brown sugar and sprinkle over breasts. Then add chicken broth and white wine. Cover with foil and bake for 1 hour at 350 degrees.

Serves: 4

Kenneth W. Crummett
Sugar Grove, West Virginia

Quail Brunch

4 quail, cleaned but not cut up
   salt
   pepper
   flour
¼ cup butter

½ cup water
6 small mushrooms
2 T. parsley, chopped
4 buttered toast slices

Sprinkle quail inside and out with salt, pepper and flour. Melt butter in a skillet and brown quail on all sides. Add water and mushrooms. Cover and cook over low heat about 10 minutes. Add parsley, cook 10 minutes longer or until tender.

Serve on buttered toast with mushroom sauce from pan, fried hominy squares or grits and applesauce.

Serves: 4

Mark J. Carlson
Newport, North Carolina

Dove and Dumplings

12 dove breasts
1 T. butter
1 tsp. sage
½ tsp. salt

½ tsp. pepper
¼ tsp. cayenne pepper
2 cups Bisquick
¾ cup milk

Brown dove breasts in butter in the bottom of a 6 quart pot. Add water to cover. Add sage, salt, pepper and cayenne pepper. Cover pot and simmer for 20 minutes.

Mix Bisquick and milk. Drop spoonfuls of batter onto surface of simmering dove breasts to form dumplings. Cover pot and allow to simmer for another 20 minutes. Dumplings will be done and dove breasts will be in a delicious gravy.

Serves: 4

Ron North
San Clemente, California

Grilled Southwestern Quail Supreme

16 quail, dressed
8 oz. Italian dressing
½ cup Chablis wine
¼ tsp. pepper
¼ tsp. salt

⅓ cup soy sauce
¼ cup lemon juice
16 quail, dressed
8 jalapeno peppers
8 slices bacon

Mix the first 6 ingredients to prepare marinade. Slice jalapeno peppers in half and put in the cavity of each quail. Wrap a piece of bacon around the bird, securing it with a toothpick. Place the birds in a bowl, cover with the marinade, and set in the refrigerator to marinate overnight or at least 8 hours.

Remove birds from marinade, remove and discard peppers. Cook on a low to medium heat grill for 15-20 minutes, turning them once during this time. Baste with marinade as desired. Serve with wild rice.

Serves: 6-8

Jim Stephens
Bartlesville, Oklahoma

Wild Turkey with Sun Dried Tomatoes and Pine Nuts

1 lb. turkey breast meat, shredded to bitesized pieces
2 T. olive oil or use oil from the sun-dried tomatoes for extra flavor
½ cup mushrooms, sliced in bitesized pieces
½ cup diced onion
½ cup diced celery, with leaves minced
¼ cup sun-dried tomatoes in olive oil, minced
1 clove garlic, minced
½ cup white or rose wine
1 T. brown sugar
¼ cup pine nuts
  salt and pepper to taste

Heat large skillet over medium high heat. When hot, add oil and turkey and cook for 2-3 minutes. Add mushrooms, onion, celery, tomatoes and garlic to the skillet. Stir fry until vegetables are about done.

Add the wine, brown sugar and pine nuts, reduce heat and simmer until liquids are reduced and turkey is done. Salt and pepper to taste. Serve with your favorite pasta or rice.

Serves: 4

Thomas H. Cedarstaff
Chesterton, Indiana

Thomas H. Cedarstaff

Wild Turkey Breast in Wine Sauce

2-3 lbs. wild turkey breast, cut
    into strips
4 T. flour
½ tsp. salt
½ tsp. pepper
2 tsp. paprika

1 tsp. sage
2 T. cooking oil
½ cup dry white wine
8 oz. fresh mushrooms, sliced
1 bunch chives chopped

Combine flour, salt, pepper, paprika and sage in a small paper or plastic bag. Add turkey breast strips and shake to coat. In a frying pan, brown turkey in hot oil. Add wine, mushrooms and onions. Cover and simmer until tender, about 45-50 minutes.

Serves: 4

Tim Goles
Houston, Texas

Roast Wild Turkey

1 wild turkey
½ cup butter

salt and pepper

Rub the inside of the turkey with butter, salt and pepper. Mix the following ingredients and stuff into cavity:

3 cups roasted peanuts
4 cups dried bread crumbs
1 egg, beaten
1 onion, finely chopped

3 tsp. butter, melted
½ cup chicken stock
½ tsp. black pepper

Place turkey in a roaster.

6-8 strips bacon

½ cup butter, melted

Lay the bacon strips over the breast. Cover the breast with cheese cloth and pour butter over the turkey so the cloth is saturated. Sprinkle with salt and pepper. Roast in oven at 350 degrees for 20 minutes per pound, basting frequently with the juices. When the bird is about done, remove the cloth to brown it a little more, if necessary.

Serves: 8

Joe Gokey
South Apopka, Florida

Partridge Supreme

4 whole partridge breasts
1 T. butter or margarine
2 cans cream of mushroom soup
1 small onion, diced
  flour
  salt

Dust the breasts in flour. Melt butter or margarine in heavy skillet and cook breasts until brown. Remove, drain and lightly sprinkle with salt. Place breasts in deep casserole and pour in soup. Sprinkle with onion. Cover and bake at 350 degrees for 70 minutes.

Serve over bed of noodles, rice or wild rice mix.

Serves: 4

Gary Somerfeld
Winnipeg, Ontario

Mr. Mac's Deep Fried Turkey Breasts

1 wild turkey breast, cut in ½" strips
2 eggs
¼ cup milk
1 tsp. lemon pepper
1 cup cornmeal

Beat eggs and milk together. Mix lemon pepper and cornmeal in a resealable plastic bag. Dip turkey in egg milk mixture, drop in cornmeal mixture and shake well to coat. Deep fry until golden brown.

Serves: 2

Thomas M. Smith
Sedalia, Missouri

Wild Grouse

3 grouse, cleaned and cut in
    serving pieces
1 egg, slightly beaten
½ cup milk
1 tsp. salt
    garlic salt to taste
1 tsp. pepper

1 cup flour
¼ cup butter
½ cup vegetable oil
1 can golden mushroom soup
1 cup water

Dip grouse pieces in mixture of egg, milk, salt, pepper and garlic salt. Roll pieces in flour. Heat butter and oil in skillet. Brown pieces well on all sides. Remove from skillet and place in a single layer in cake pan. Add drippings from skillet to mushroom soup and mix well. Spoon over grouse pieces. Add water to cake pan. Cover with foil and bake at 350 degrees for 1 hour or until tender.

Serves: 4

William Soltis
Saginaw, Michigan

Ringneck Casserole

2 ringneck pheasants
¼ lb. butter
2 T. sherry
1 clove garlic, mashed
2 stalks celery, diced
1 onion, chopped
½ cup black olives

1 cup mushrooms, sliced
1 pkg. bread stuffing mix
½ cup sour cream
1 cup chicken broth
1 cup half and half
2 T. parsley, chopped

Cut 2 pheasants into pieces the size of your big toe. Saute in butter with sherry and garlic. Add the rest of the ingredients except parsley. Toss gently to mix liquids and flavor. Place in buttered casserole. Sprinkle parsley over top. Cover and bake at 325 degrees for 1 hour.

Serves: 8

Karen Pennaz
Maple Plain, Minnesota

Wild Rice
Spinach Bake

1 mediun onion
1 pkg. frozen chopped spinach,
   thawed and drained
2 cups grated cheddar cheese

1½ cups cooked wild rice
3 eggs, beaten until frothy
1 cup milk
1 tsp. salt

Combine the onion, spinach, cheese and wild rice. Blend. Mix the eggs, milk and salt and stir into the spinch and wild rice mixture. Pour into a lightly greased 1½ quart casserole.

Set this in a pan with enough hot water to come up the sides of the casserole about an inch. Bake at 350 degrees for 50-60 minutes or until the casserol is set in the middle. This also makes a filling and hearty main dish.

Serves: 8-10

Karen Pennaz
Maple Plain, Minnesota

Cherry Dump Camp Cobbler

1 box yellow cake mix
½ cup crushed cornflakes mix
1 large can cherry pie filling
1 large can crushed pineapple
1½ sticks margarine, melted
1 cup crushed pecans

Combine yellow cake mix and crushed cornflakes in a bowl. Grease 9" x 11" rectangular cake pan and spoon in cherries and spread, then dump in crushed pineapple and spread. Next spoon cake/cornflake mixture on top of this and pack slightly. Then pur melted margarine on top of this and pack slightly. Then pour melted margarine on top evenly. Next sprinkle pecans on top. Bake for 1 hour at 325 degrees and watch pecans carefully near the end, they burn quickly.

Serves: 12

Laura Seitz
Golden Eagle Archery

Waterfowl

Coots
Ducks

Goose Ravioli

Filling

- 1 cup leftover goose, ground
- 2 eggs
- ¼ cup Italian seasoned bread crumbs
- ½ cup grated Parmesan cheese
    salt and pepper to taste

Mix above ingredients, then add enough goose stock or gravy to form a stiff paste.

Dough

- 1 pound flour
- 5 eggs

Pour out flour onto a cutting board and make well in center. Beat eggs, carefully pour into well and slowly mix eggs into flour. If too dry, add small amount of olive oil or water. If sticky, add small amount of flour. Knead until smooth and soft. Wrap in towel and allow to rest 15 minutes.

Roll out a sheet of dough until it's ⅛" thick. Place on floured board and cut with knife or pizza cutter into 2 equal long strips about 3" wide. Partly score one strip to mark 3" squares. Place about a tablespoon of filling in center of each square. Place another strip along top of the strip containing the meat mixture and gently press down with fingers to seal the filling firmly on four sides in separate little mounds. With a pie jagger, first cut along the lengthwise edges of the strips to reinforce the side closures. Then cut between the strips to seal separate the individual raviolis. Put the squares on a rack to dry 1-2 hours.

Drop raviolis in salted water or broth until done and cook until done, about 5 minutes. Remove with spoon and drain. Place 6-8 raviolis on each serving plate and top with spaghetti sauce and Parmesan cheese.

Serves: 4

Janice Anderson
Morton, Illinois

Marinated Goose Breast

2 goose breasts
¾ cup red wine
¼ cup soy sauce
¼ cup corn syrup

1 medium onion, sliced finely
1 clove garlic, crushed
⅓ cup vegetable oil

Combine all the ingredients except the oil and goose breasts in a large bowl. Slice the goose breasts lengthwise to make 4 thin fillets. Pierce both sides of breasts with a fork. Brush the vegetable oil on the breasts and let sit for about 1 hour. Place the breasts in the marinade mix and let sit overnight in the refrigerator.

Drain the breasts on paper towel. Cook on a hot charcoal or gas grill. Take care to only cook until center is warm. The meat will be dry if overcooked. The meat can also be cut into chunks and used as kabobs.

Serves: 4
Jim Simpson
Manchester, Missouri

WATERFOWL

Grilled Canadian Goose

1 Canadian goose
½ cup olive oil
½ cup soy sauce
½ cup brown sugar

½ cup thawed orange juice concentrate
½ cup honey dijon mustard
¼ cup honey

Mix the oil, soy sauce, brown sugar, orange juice and mustard in a bowl. Cut the goose into chunks or slice about 1" thick. Pour the marinade over the goose pieces in a shallow glass pan and marinate for about 4 hours, stirring occasionally. Remove the goose and drain on paper towels.

Mix some honey with 1 cup of the reserved marinade. Grill goose pieces over medium heat for approximately 20 minutes. Baste with marinade.

Serves: 8

Mike McCartney
Oxford, Ohio

Zeman's Wild Duck Creole

2 wild ducks
2 onions
1 T. flour
2 T. butter or margarine, melted
2 slices raw bacon
4 small onions

4 carrots
3 parsley sprigs, chopped
2 cups tomato juice
2 cups consomme
  juice of 1 orange
  salt and pepper

Rub ducks inside and out with salt and place in deep baking dish. Put one onion inside each. Mix flour with melted butter and rub over breast of birds. Lay slice of bacon on top of each bird. Place in roasting pan and bake in hot oven (400-450 degrees) for 15 minutes. Add the onions, carrots and chopped parsley.

In a sauce pan, combine tomato juice, orange juice and consomme. Bring to a boil and add salt and pepper. Pour over birds and bake, covered for 45 minutes at 350 degrees. Birds will still be rare. If very rare bird is desired, cook only 30 minutes.

Serves: 4

Helen Zeman
Memphis, Tennessee

Wild Ducks and Turnips

2 wild ducks, cleaned and
    cut in pieces
2 turnips, quartered
2 T. butter

2 onions, chopped
1 bay leaf
1 T. flour

Melt butter in Dutch oven. Add onions and cook until wilted. Add the ducks and season to taste. Cook slowly until brown. Add turnips and sifted flour, stirring constantly until lightly brown. Add bay leaf and cook for 15 minutes, stirring regularly. Then add water to nearly cover ducks and stir well. Cover tightly and simmer for about 30 minutes or until tender.

Serves: 4

Clyde H. Arnold
Port Allen, Louisiana

Wild Duck Gumbo

2 ducks, cut up
½ cup oil
⅔ cup flour
1 lb. smoked sausage, sliced
2 cups onion, chopped
1½ cups green pepper, chopped
1½ cups celery, chopped
2½ T. garlic, minced
1 14½-oz. can stewed tomatoes
2 bay leaves
2 T. Worcestershire sauce
1½ tsp. pepper
1 tsp. salt
1 tsp. dried thyme
1¼ tsp. cayenne pepper
2 quarts water
hot cooked rice

In a Dutch oven, brown duck in oil. Remove and set aside. Keep ⅔ cup drippings and add flour. Cook and stir until brown. Add sausage, onion, green pepper, celery and garlic. Cook 10 minutes, stirring occasionally. Add next 8 ingredients and mix well. Add duck and bring to boil. Reduce heat and cover, simmer about 1 hour, until duck is tender. Remove duck and debone. Return duck to pan and simmer about 10 minutes. Remove bay leaves and serve with rice.

Serves: 4

Lynn Strickland
Hampton, Arizona

Grilled Duck Breasts with Red Currant Sauce

4-6 whole duck breasts

Marinade

2 T. soy sauce
½ tsp. dry mustard
1 T. Worcestershire sauce
¼ tsp. garlic powder
¾ cup dry red wine

Remove meat in one piece from both sides of breast bone. Remove skin and trim tendons. In large bowl, combine all marinade ingredients. Add duck, turning to coat all sides. Marinate in refrigerator for at least 4 hours or overnight.

Red Currant Sauce

4 T. unsalted butter
1 10-oz. jar red currant jelly
¼ cup ketchup
¼ cup brown sugar, packed

Melt butter in small sauce pan. Stir in jelly, ketchup and brown sugar. Heat until jelly melts and mixture boils.

Grill breasts for 5 minutes per side. Meat should be rare to medium rare. Carve into ¼" slices, cutting across grain. Serve with red currant sauce.

Serves: 4-6

Chris Wilkinson
Lamar, Colorado

Ducks on the Pond

8 ducks, breast and legs (skinned)
   salt and pepper to taste
   flour (as needed)
2 sticks butter
2 medium yellow onions, sliced
2 medium bell peppers, sliced
2 stalks celery, sliced
1 clove garlic, minced

3 cans chicken broth
¼ bottle Worcestershire sauce
1 bottle hot sauce
2 small cans mushrooms
4 oz. wine

Salt, pepper and flour ducks well. Brown ducks in butter. Set aside. Cook onions, bell pepper, celery and garlic until onions are clear. Add ducks, broth, Worcestershire sauce, hot pepper and simmer for 3½ hours. Add mushrooms and wine; simmer for ½ hour longer. Serve over rice.

Serves: 8-10

Linus Hawkins
Jennings, Louisiana

WATERFOWL

Baked Wild Duck

1 duck
1½ T. butter
1 pkg. dried onion soup mix

Place 1 tablespoon butter over the breast and ½ tablespoon inside of bird. Spread 2 tablespoons soup mix on the breast and 1 tablespoon on the inside. Wrap tightly in foil, breast side up. Bake at 425 degrees for 40 minutes.

Serves: 2

Leslie E. Beaton
Eugene, Oregon

Goose Kabobs

1 goose
1 cup red wine vinegar
2 cups water
½ cup brown sugar
¼ cup salt
2 T. soy sauce
2 T. garlic powder
2 green peppers, cut into bitesized pieces
2 red onions, cut into bitesized pieces

Breast out goose, with thighs attached. For marinade, mix red wine vinegar, water, brown sugar, salt, soy sauce and garlic powder together. Add goose and marinate overnight.

Cut goose into bite size pieces. Thread on skewers alternating peppers, onion and meat. Barbecue on grill, cover grill with tin foil or use cookie sheet.

Mix the following sauce ingredients together and brush kabobs while grilling:

2 sticks butter, melted
2 T. garlic powder
1 T. lemon pepper
1 tsp. coarse black pepper
2 T. salt

Serves: 2-4

Greg Lattery
St. Paul, Minnesota

Roast Wild Goose

1 goose	margarine
salt	bacon
2 apples	flour
leaves from celery stalks	

Clean the goose and wipe the cavity dry with paper towels. Rub a little salt on the inside. Put in a couple of peeled, cored and quartered apples and the leaves from several stalks of celery. Place the stuffed bird in a roasting pan, breast side up. Rub a little margarine over the breast or lay several strips of bacon across it, as geese tend to be dry at times. Roast at 325 degrees, basting with pan juices occasionally.

After 1½ hours, begin testing for doneness by squeezing the thigh with a folded paper towel. If it yields to pressure, it is done. Stir a little flour into the pan juices after you have removed the fowl to a heated platter. Add water, a little at a time, until you have a gravy just thick enough to suit your taste.

Serves: 6-8

Robert G. Hopfer
Pennsylvania

Baked Goose

5 lb. goose, legs or breasts
1 16-oz. can sauerkraut
   salt and pepper to taste
8 oz. ranch dressing
8 oz. Swiss cheese

Put goose in a greased 13" x 9" x 2" glass baking dish. Put sauerkraut on goose and add salt and pepper to taste. Pour dressing over top. Top with cheese. Cover with foil and bake at 350 degrees for 1½ hours or until done.

Serves: 4-6

Lewis Drullinger and Jody Brown
Woodston, Kansas

Golden Goose

2 Canada goose breast fillets	1 can golden mushroom soup
1 stick butter or margarine	¼ cup water
2-3 T. flour	1 bay leaf
½ tsp. salt	½ tsp. juniper berries
¼ tsp. lemon pepper seasoning	½ tsp. pickling spice

Slice breast fillets into thin strips. Melt butter or margarine in frying pan. Combine flour, salt and lemon pepper in a shallow plate or pan (soup bowl or pie plate). Roll goose strips in seasoned flour and brown in butter or margarine. Remove browned goose strips from frying pan and place on paper towel to absorb excess butter.

Pour soup in Crockpot and dilute with water. Add browned goose strips. Put bay leaf, juniper berries and pickling spice in a small cheesecloth bag and add to Crockpot. Cook on low 4-6 hours or until goose is tender. Serve over egg dumpling noodles.

Serves: 4

Judy Brennan
Wausau, Wisconsin

Rice Stuffed Wild Goose

1 large goose	2 cans chicken broth
¼ cup butter	1 tsp. parsley
2 cups uncooked rice	½ tsp. thyme
½ cup chopped onion	½ tsp. pepper
½ cup chopped celery	4-6 bacon slices
1 can mushrooms	

To make stuffing, melt butter in large pan. Add rice, onion, celery and mushrooms. Saute until rice is lightly browned. Add chicken broth, parsley, thyme and pepper. Cover and let simmer for 20 minutes or until rice is tender. Remove from heat and let sit until stuffing is cool enough to handle.

Stuff goose and place in a roasting pan with the breast side up. Cover breast with bacon slices and roast for 25-30 minutes per pound.

Serves: 6-8

Ed Agentowicz
Clarks Summit, Pennsylvania

Sweet-Sour Fillet of Duck

4 boneless duck breasts, butterflied
   flour
   cooking oil
1 small can pineapple tidbits
2 T. soy sauce

1 T. corn starch
1 cup cold water
1 medium green bell pepper, cut into
   bitesized pieces

Prepare duck breast by butterflying the fillet. Dredge in flour to coat and brown quickly in a very hot skillet with a small amount of oil. Remove from pan.

Drain pineapple and put juice in a small saucepan. Add soy sauce and cornstarch mixed in cold water. Cook over medium heat, stirring constantly until mixture thickens. Add pineapple and green pepper.

Return duck to skillet, pour sauce over breasts and heat just until bubbling. Serve over rice or Oriental noodles.

Serves: 4

Ted Horton
Grand Rapids, Minnesota

Duck un Kraut

4-5 lb. duckling
   salt
   pepper
2 quarts sauerkraut
1 cup water
3 T. sugar

1½ cups white wine
⅛ tsp. nutmeg
   salt and pepper
2 celery stalks and leaves, chopped
2 cups apples, cored and chopped

Clean and rinse duck; pat dry with paper towels. Rub inside with salt and pepper. Place in a roasting pan. Add sauerkraut, water and sugar. Cover and cook at 350 degrees until duck is tender and golden brown. Allow 20-25 minutes per pound.

Serve with creamy mashed potatoes. If desired, the sauerkraut may be used as a stuffing. Allow 1 pound of duck per serving.

Serves: 4-6

Joseph Adamick
Pottsville, Pennsylvania

Bacon Duck

1 duck
3 cups cubed, dried bread
1 tsp. sage
1 tsp. salt
1-2 tsp. pepper
1 stalk chopped celery

1 T. minced onion
1 egg
1 cup water
¼ cup butter (melted)
4 slices bacon

Place cubes of bread in large bowl, then sprinkle on sage, salt, pepper, celery and onion. Now mix together egg, water and butter and pour over bread mixture to moisten. If too dry, add more water. Stuff dressing in cavity and wrap duck in bacon strips, holding in place with toothpicks. Place in roaster in 325 degree oven for approximately 1½ hours. Keep an eye on it.

Serves: 4

Paul F. Burns
Greenville, Pennsylvania

Wild Goose Okie Style

1 goose, cleaned
2 apples peeled, cored, quartered
2 small onions, peeled and quartered
2 cups sliced mushrooms
4 T. butter

1 cup sherry
salt
pepper
paprika

Prick goose skin several times. Stuff cavity with apples and onions. Roast in a 500 degree oven, uncovered, for 30 minutes.

Meanwhile, saute mushrooms and butter until warm. Remove goose from oven, turn oven down to 350 degrees and pour mushrooms and butter over goose. Pour sherry over goose. Lightly season with salt, pepper and paprika. Cover and return to the oven for an additional 1-2 hours, until tender. Drippings will make excellent gravy.

Serves: 6-8

Gerry Dilschneider
Henryetta, Oklahoma

Wild Duck Dressing

4 cups fresh or canned sauerkraut
2 cups chopped sweet onion
2 cups chopped apples (Jonathan
    or Granny)
½ cup grated potato
1 T. caraway seed
    pinch of salt
½ tsp. coarse ground pepper

1½ cups white wine
⅛ tsp. nutmeg
    salt and pepper
2 celery stalks and leaves, chopped
2 cups apples, cored and chopped

Mix ingredients together for delicious duck stuffing.

Ernest Schmidt
Kearney, Nebraska

Mike's Roast Goose

1 young goose
⅓ cup vinegar
    juice of 2 lemons
    juice of 1 orange
1 small bay leaf
2 sprigs parsley

Clean, wash and pat the goose dry. Combine vinegar, lemon juice, orange juice, bay leaf, parsley, white wine and nutmeg. Add goose and marinate for 3-4 hours, turning and basting frequently. Remove goose from marinade and rub cavity with salt and pepper. Place celery and apples inside.

Truss goose and place breast side up in a roasting pan. Sear for 20 minutes in a very hot oven (450 degrees). Turn goose breast side down, cover pan and lower heat to 350 degrees. Continue roasting for 1-1½ hours, basting with marinade and pan drippings.

Serves: 6-8

Mike Rasmussen
Burnsville, Minnesota

Husker Roast Duck

1 young duck
2 cups peeled, quartered apples
1 onion slice
2 tsp. salt
¼ tsp. pepper
1 cup orange juice

Fill cavity of duck with apples. Close with skewers and tie legs and wings close to body. Rub duck with slice of onion, followed by salt and pepper. Roast uncovered at 325 degrees for 1½-2 hours. Baste every 10 minutes with orange juice.

Serves: 2-4

Mel Huffman
Decatur, Nebraska

Wild Garlic Duck

1 duck, chooked

Stuff duck with:

1 orange, quartered
1 apple, quartered

1 small onion, quartered
1 stalk celery, chopped

Spread or brush duck with:

2-3 T. garlic jelly

Mix together:

1 tsp. sage
1 tsp. thyme
1 tsp. basil
½ tsp. paprika

½ tsp. oregano
1 tsp. salt
½ tsp. lemon pepper

Dust spices over duck. Bake at 350 degrees for 1-1½ hours, depending on weight.

Serves: 4

James Wallace
Sylmar, California

Duck with Oyster Sauce

3 duck breasts

Marinade

¼ cup red wine
1 T. soy sauce
⅛ tsp. MSG
   pinch of 5-spice powder
2 T. peanut oil
1 clove garlic, minced
1 medium onion, sliced

1 stalk celery, sliced
½ green pepper, sliced
2 cups fresh mushrooms, sliced
½ cup chicken broth
1 medium tomato, sliced

Oyster Sauce

2 T. oyster sauce
1 T. cornstarch
¼ cup water
   salt and pepper to taste

Slice duck into bite size pieces and put in bowl. Mix marinade ingredients together and pour over duck. Let sit for 1 hour. Drain before cooking.

Heat pan. Add oil and garlic. Stir fry for a few seconds. Add duck, stir fry on medium heat for 5 minutes. Turn heat down to low, add splash of wine. Cover and steam for 10 minutes.

Uncover, turn heat up, add onion, celery, green pepper and mushrooms. Stir fry 1 minute; add salt and pepper to taste. Add chicken broth, stir, cover and steam for 3 minutes.

Mix oyster sauce ingredients together. Uncover duck and add tomato and oyster sauce. Stir fry until done. Serve over rice.

Serves: 4

Ryan Thorsness
Baudette, Minnesota

Lawry's
Wild Game Recipes

LAWRY'S®

Chef Eric's Poached Quail in Vegetable Broth

12 quail with rib cage and thigh bone removed
1 cup Lawry's Mesquite with Lime Juice Marinade
¼ tsp. black pepper
½ lb. bacon, diced
1 onion, diced
2 stalks fresh fennel, cored and sliced

2 quarts chicken stock
1 bay leaf
2 small russet potatoes, peeled and thinly sliced
1 8¾-oz. can kernel corn
1 leek, sliced
2 cloves garlic, minced
Lawry's Seasoned Salt
white pepper

In resealable plastic bag, combine quail, Mesquite with Lime Juice Marinade and black pepper. Seal bag and refrigerate 2 hours.

In large stock pot, saute bacon and onion until onions are caramelized (will be brown in color). Add fennel, chicken stock, bay leaf and marinated quail. Simmer, uncovered, 50 minutes or until quail are tender. Remove quail from stock; set aside.

Add potato and corn to stock. Simmer, uncovered, 5 minutes. Add leek, garlic, Seasoned Salt and white pepper, to taste. Simmer, uncovered, an additional 3-4 minutes.

Red Bell Pepper Sauce

1 14-oz. jar roasted red bell peppers
½ tsp. Lawry's Garlic Powder with Parsley
¼ cup Lawry's Mesquite with Lime Juice Marinade
2 limes, cut into wedges (garnish)

In blender, combine red bell pepper, Garlic Powder with Parsley and Mesquite with Lime Juice Marinade. Blend on medium for 15-30 seconds.

Presentation: Place 2 quail in serving bowl. Add stock and vegetables, about 1½ cups, distributing vegetables as evenly as possible. Drizzle with Red Bell Pepper Sauce.

Serves: 6

Eric A. Widmer, Contributing Chef

172

Venison Taco Salad

- 1 lb. ground venison
- 1 pkg. (1.25 oz) Lawry's Taco Spices & Seasonings
- 1 head lettuce, shredded
- 2 cups mild Cheddar cheese, grated
- ½ cup pitted black olives, sliced
- 2 tomatoes, cut in small pieces
- ½ medium onion, chopped
- 1 cup Thousand Island salad dressing
- 8 oz. tortilla chips

In large skillet, cook venison until brown. Drain any excess fat. Stir in Taco Spices and Seasonings. Refrigerate meat until well chilled.

In large bowl, combine seasoned venison, lettuce, Cheddar cheese, olives, tomatoes and onions. Add dressing and chips; blend well.

Serves: 8-10

Paula J. Del Guidice, Nevada Editor
OUTDOOR LIFE

LAWRY'S

Lemon Pepper and Pineapple Quail

4 small game birds - quail, chukar, grouse, etc.
    (1-2 birds per person)
1 12-oz. bottle Lawry's Lemon Pepper with Lemon Juice

Marinade

⅔ cup packed brown sugar
    prepared stuffing mix
    Lawry's Lemon Pepper

2 cups pineapple chunks
    butter
    mint leaves (garnish)

In small bowl, combine Lemon Pepper with Lemon Juice Marinade and brown sugar; blend well to dissolve sugar. In resealable plastic bag, combine marinade mixture and game birds. Seal bag and refrigerate 2 hours, turning occasionally. Sprinkle cavity of birds with Lemon Pepper.

Using your favorite bird stuffing (wild rice and mushroom is excellent), stuff, truss and place birds, breast side down, in baking pan. Place a few dots of butter on top of birds. Pour remaining marinade over birds. Bake at 350 degrees for 1½-2 hours. Baste occasionally with pan juices. Add pineapple last half hour of cooking. If birds need browning, leave uncovered at this time and raise oven temperature to 400 degrees.

Presentation: Serve birds whole with pineapple arranged around the bird. Pour a little of the pan juices over the top and serve remainder in a small pitcher or side dish. Garnish with mint leaves.

Serves: 2-4

Ed and Lue Park, Oregon Editor
OUTDOOR LIFE

Grilled Venison Steaks Lawry's

2 lbs. venison or antelope steaks
⅓ cup Lawry's Teriyaki with
    Pineapple Juice Marinade
½ cup Lawry's Mesquite with Lime
    Juice Marinade
⅓ cup soy sauce
Lawry's Garlic Powder with Parsley
black pepper

Pound venison steaks with meat hammer to tenderize. Sprinkle Garlic Powder with Parsley on one side of steaks only. Sprinkle freshly ground black pepper on other side of steaks. Rub both sides of steaks with small amount of soy sauce and Teriyaki with Pineapple Juice Marinade. Set steaks aside for 1 hour in refrigerator to marinate.

Remove steaks from refrigerator and brush Mesquite with Lime Juice Marinade on both sides of meat, rubbing in with fingers. Let marinated steaks stand an additional 2 hours in refrigerator.

Grill over medium heat, 7-10 minutes, turning once.

Presentation: Serve with baked potatoes.

Serves: 4-6

Sam and Nancy Fadala, Outdoor Writer
Casper, Wyoming

LAWRY'S

"Mission Impossible" Duck or Goose

Fillet meat from 1 duck or goose
1 12-oz. bottle Lawry's Lemon Pepper with Lemon Juice Marinade
Horseradish sauce

Pound fillets with meat hammer to tenderize. In resealable plastic bag, combine fillets and Lemon Pepper with Lemon Juice Marinade. Seal bag and refrigerate 2 hours, turning occasionally.

Grill fillets over hot coals, turning after 5-10 minutes. Cook an additional 5-10 minutes. Do not over cook.

Presentation: Slice fillets thinly and serve with horseradish sauce.

Serves: 4

Charlie Farmer, Outdoor Writer
Ozark, Michigan

Grilled Venison Chops

8 venison chops or tenderloin, cut into 1½" thick slices
1 12-oz. bottle Lawry's Teriyaki with Pineapple Juice Marinade
Lawry's Garlic Powder with Parsley

In resealable plastic bag, combine chops and marinade. Seal bag and refrigerate 3 hours. Spray grill with cooking spray. Grill 5-7 minutes on each side. Baste with leftover marinade and sprinkle with Garlic Powder with Parsley while cooking, turning once. Do not over cook.

Presentation: Serve with baked potato and fresh tossed salad.

Serves: 6-8

Tom and Betty Lou Fegely
Outdoor Writers

Dove Kabob Teriyaki

12   whole dove breasts, skinned
1 12-oz. bottle Lawry's Teriyaki with Pineapple Juice Marinade
2 white onions, cut into chunks
4 tomatoes, cut into chunks
1 green bell pepper, cut into chunks
1 red bell pepper, cut into chunks
1 yellow squash, cut into chunks
Lawry's Seasoned Salt
Lawry's Garlic Pepper

In resealable plastic bag, combine dove breasts and Teriyaki with Pineapple Juice Marinade. Seal bag and refrigerate 2 hours.

On skewers, alternate dove breast pieces with vegetable chunks. Sprinkle with Seasoned Salt and Garlic Pepper to taste. Broil kabobs on grill, brushing continually with marinade. Do not over cook.

Presentation: Serve over rice.

Serves: 6-8

Bob Saile
Outdoor Editor, DENVER POST

Javelina Loin with Mushroom and Pine Nut Sauce

    2 lbs. javelina loin, cut into 4 serving size pieces
    1 12-oz. bottle Lawry's Red Wine with Cabernet Sauvignon Marinade
    1 cup butter or margarine
    1 lb. fresh mushrooms, sliced
       Lawry's Seasoned Salt
       Lawry's Garlic Pepper
    ¼ cup Burgundy wine

In resealable plastic bag, combine javelina loin and 1¼ cups Red Wine with Cabernet Sauvignon Marinade and refrigerate for at least 2 hours or overnight.

In large skillet, melt ½ cup butter. Saute garlic and mushrooms; set aside. Drain loin and saute in the same skillet, adding Seasoned Salt and Garlic Pepper to taste. Add Burgundy wine and ¼ cup Red Wine with Cabernet Sauvignon Marinade during the last minute of cooking time. Return mushrooms to the pan to reheat.

Pine Nut Sauce

    ½ cup butter or margarine
    ½ cup whole pine nuts
       Lawry's Seasoned Salt
    1-2 tsp. cornstarch
       Lawry's Lemon Pepper

In large skillet, melt butter or margarine. Add pine nuts and saute. Add Seasoned Salt and Lemon Pepper to taste. Stir in 1 teaspoon cornstarch; blend well and heat to thicken. Add additional cornstarch, ½ teaspoon at a time; bring to a boil until glaze is desired thickness.

Presentation: Remove meat and mushrooms to preheated plates; drizzle with pan juices and Pine Nut Sauce. Serve with wild rice and your favorite vegetable.

Serves: 4-6

Bob Hirsch, Outdoor Writer
Cave Creek, Arizona

Bob's Venison Stew

4 lbs. venison, cut into chunks
2 quarts or 2 16-oz. cans tomatoes
2 beef bouillon cubes
3 cups water
2 cloves garlic, minced
1½ T. Italian seasoning
1 T. Lawry's Seasoned Salt
1 T. Worcestershire sauce
2 tsp. sweet basil
1 16-oz. pkg. frozen stir fry vegetables
1 8-oz. can sliced water chestnuts or bamboo shoots
  Lawry's Seasoned Salt
  Lawry's Garlic Pepper
  sesame seed oil

In large roasting pan, brown venison without fat. After red color is gone, add remaining ingredients. If meat is tender, let simmer 1-1½ hours. If you know venison may be tough, simmer 2-2½ hours. Add more water if necessary and stir occasionally.

Presentation: Serve with warm bread.

Serves: 6-8

Bob Schrank, Field Reporter
OUTDOOR NEWS

Roasted Wild Duck

2 mallard ducks, plucked
2 T. butter or margarine
1 cup water
1 tsp. ground sage
1 medium onion, half chopped and half sliced
2 cups croutons
4 strips bacon
½ cup blush wine
   Lawry's Seasoned Salt
   Lawry's Seasoned Pepper

Rub duck inside and out with Seasoned Salt and Seasoned Pepper. In large sauce pan, melt butter and ½ cup water; add ground sage and ¼ cup chopped onion. Mix with croutons; blend well.

Stuff birds loosely. Line bottom of roasting pan with sliced onion. Place birds breast-up in pan and cover each with 2 strips bacon. Add ½ cup water and ½ cup wine to bottom of pan. Cover and bake at 300 degrees for 2 hours, or until tender.

Presentation: Serve with mixed vegetables and potatoes.

LAWRY'S

Serves: 4

Roger Sparks, Editor
WILDFOWL

Heart Healthy Fajitas

2-3 lbs. venison roast
1 12-oz. bottle Lawry's Lemon
   Pepper with Lemon Juice
   Marinade
3 bell peppers, sliced (green,
   yellow or red)

2 large onions, sliced
20 flour tortillas, warmed
   Lawry's Seasoned Salt
   Lawry's Lemon Pepper
   Lawry's Garlic Powder with Parsley

Trim any excess fat and silver skin from meat. Slice into bite sized pieces or strips. In resealable plastic bag, combine meat and Lemon Pepper with Lemon Juice Marinade. Seal bag and refrigerate 3 hours or overnight.

In large skillet, place meat and marinade. Bring to boil; reduce heat and simmer until cooked. Remove meat from skillet, leaving excess marinade.

Lightly saute onions and bell peppers in remaining marinade. Cook until semi-crisp. Combine vegetables and meat. Season to taste with Seasoned Salt, Lemon Pepper and Garlic Powder with Parsley.

Presentation: Spoon mixture into tortillas, fold and enjoy.

Serves: 8-10

Debbie and Pat Wray, Outdoor Writer
Corvallis, Oregon

The Easiest (and Best) of All Venison Recipes

2 lbs. venison loin
1 12-oz. bottle Lawry's Mesquite
   with Lime Juice Marinade
1 T. olive oil

1 T. minced garlic
   Lawry's Seasoned Salt
   Lawry's Garlic Pepper

Cut loin into 1" thick rounds (or slice roast or steaks). In a resealable plastic bag or glass dish, combine meat and Mesquite Marinade and refrigerate for several hours or overnight.

Drain meat and sprinkle with Seasoned Salt and Garlic Pepper. Mix olive oil and minced garlic in frying pan and heat until very hot. Add meat and cook quickly, turning once. Meat should be pink in the middle. Remove to pre-heated plates and top with pan juices.

Presentation: Serve with wild rice and spaghetti squash in butter.

Serves: 4

Bob Hirsch, Outdoor Writer
Cave Creek, Arizona

Stuffed Venison Steaks Ole!

If you're after tender venison with a hint of Old Mexico, this is the way to go. Guaranteed to enhance your reputation as a top wild game chef!

- 3 lbs. venison steak, pounded to ¼" thickness
- 3 T. butter or margarine
- 2 stalks celery, chopped
- 1 cup onion, diced
- 1 green pepper, diced
- 2 cups dry bread crumbs
- ½ tsp. Lawry's Seasoned Salt
- ¼ tsp. Lawry's Garlic Pepper
- 1 1.25-oz. pkg. Lawry's Taco Spices and Seasonings
- 1 12-oz. bottle Lawry's Seasoned Marinade

Melt butter in saucepan and saute celery, onion and green pepper. Mix in a bowl with bread crumbs, Seasoned Salt and Garlic Pepper, adding a little water if needed to make a moist dressing. Place the mixture on each steak, roll and fasten with toothpicks. Brown stuffed steaks in an oiled skillet.

Mix Taco Spices and Seasonings with Seasoned Marinade, pour over steaks and simmer slowly for one hour. The steaks can also be baked in a dish in the oven at 350 degrees for 1 hour.

LAWRY'S

Serves: 8

Bob Hirsch, Outdoor Writer
Cave Creek, Arizona

Crunchy Cottontail

2 lbs. rabbit
1 12-oz. bottle Lawry's Herb and Garlic with Lemon Juice

Marinade

1 cup crushed cornflakes
1 tsp. Lawry's Seasoned Salt
¼ tsp. Lawry's Garlic Powder
⅛ tsp. Lawry's Lemon Pepper
   butter
1 tsp. paprika

Cut rabbit into serving pieces and marinate with Herb and Garlic with Lemon Juice Marinade in a bowl or resealable plastic bag, refrigerated, for 2 hours. Remove and drain.

In a paper bag, combine crushed cornflakes, Seasoned Salt, Garlic Powder and Lemon Pepper. Add one piece of rabbit at a time and shake well to coat. Place meat in shallow baking dish, dot with butter and sprinkle with paprika. Bake at 350 degrees for 1 hour.

Serves: 4

Bob Hirsch, Outdoor Writer
Cave Creek, Arizona

Venison Meatball (Albondigas) Soup

In Mexico, albondigas soup is a favorite hangover cure but it's delicious for those who don't imbibe as well. The recipe is for 8-10 servings because the soup is even better when reheated the second day.

- 2 lbs. lean ground venison
- 3 quarts water
- 1 14-oz. can tomato sauce
- 2 medium tomatoes, diced
- 1 4-oz. can diced green chilies
- 2 cloves garlic
- 1 bunch fresh cilantro, chopped
- 3 green onions, chopped
- 1 cup uncooked rice
- 2 T. flour
  Lawry's Seasoned Salt
  Lawry's Garlic Pepper

Bring water to a boil and add tomato sauce, tomatoes, green chilies, garlic, half of the cilantro and half of the green onions. Lower heat and simmer.

LAWRY'S

In a large bowl, mix ground venison with rice, flour, Seasoned Salt, Garlic Pepper and the remainder of the cilantro and onions. Bring the soup back to a boil, form meatballs (albondigas!) and drop them into the boiling soup. When the meatballs float to the top, the soup is done.

Presentation: Serve with warm tortillas and lemon or lime wedges. And let the individual eaters add hot sauce to their bowl if they like it "muy spicy".

Serves: 8-10

Bob Hirsch, Outdoor Writer
Cave Creek, Arizona

Sauteed Quail
A La Marinade

12 whole quail, Bobwhite or Western species	1 tsp. Lawry's Garlic Salt with Parsley
1 12-oz. bottle Lawry's Mesquite with Lime Juice Marinade	2 medium onions, sliced or 6 shallots, diced
3 T. butter	1 lb. fresh mushrooms, sliced

In resealable plastic bag, combine quail and Mesquite with Lime Juice Marinade. Seal bag and refrigerate 4 hours or overnight, turning occasionally.

In large skillet, melt butter. Add onions, sprinkle with Garlic Salt with Parsley and saute 5 minutes. Add marinated quail; cook 5 minutes over medium high heat, turning frequently. Add mushrooms and cook additional 5 minutes. Do not over cook.

Presentation: Serve over rice.

Serves: 4

Tom Huggler,
Outdoor Writer

Stir Fry Duck Breast

4 whole ducks, skinned or plucked	1 medium white onion, diced
1 12-oz. bottle Lawry's Teriyaki with Pineapple Juice Marinade	2 cups diced carrots
	2 cups diced celery

In resealable plastic bag, combine ducks and Teriyaki with Pineapple Juice Marinade, reserving ¼ cup marinade. Seal bag and refrigerate 2 hours.

Fillet breast meat and dice it. In wok, saute diced duck breasts in 2 tablespoons of Teriyaki with Pineapple Juice Marinade; add Seasoned Salt and Garlic Pepper to taste. Add vegetables and stir fry until vegetables are tender crisp. Add a few shakes of sesame seed oil and drizzle reserved ¼ cup Teriyaki with Pineapple Juice Marinade over vegetables. Cook additional minute.

Presentation: Serve over rice.

Serves: 4

Bob Hirsch, Outdoor Writer
Cave Creek, Arizona

Delicious Duck

   2 ducks
   ½ cup flour
   2 tsp. sage
   1 tsp. Lawry's Seasoned Salt
   1 tsp. Lawry's Garlic Pepper
   ¼ lb. butter
   1 onion, chopped
   3 stalks celery, chopped
   ½ lb. fresh mushrooms, sliced
   1 tsp. Lawry's Garlic Powder with Parsley
   1 tsp. thyme

Debone duck breasts and cut into bite size pieces. Dredge meat in a mixture of flour, sage, Seasoned Salt and Garlic Pepper and brown in a skillet with butter. Remove breasts and add onion, celery and mushrooms and saute. Add breasts, plus Garlic Powder and thyme; cover and simmer on low heat for 1 hour.

Presentation: Serve with rice and buttered carrots.

Serves: 4

Bob Hirsch, Outdoor Writer
Cave Creek, Arizona

LAWRY'S

Indexes

Recipes

A

Alligator Italian Style, 127
Arabian Stew, 82

B

Bacon Duck, 166
Bagged Venison Roast, 18
Baked Coon and Onion, 132
Baked Goose, 163
Baked Rabbit Italiano, 136
Baked Wild Duck, 161
Barbecue Raccoon, 132
Barbecued Antelope, 122
Barbecued Elk Ribs, 108
Barbecued Meatballs, 47
Barbecued Venison Ribs, 40
Batter Fried Partridge, 140
Bear Chops, 121
Bear Dumpling Stew, 115
Bear's Quail and Wild Rice, 144
Bill Miller's Wild Game Steak Recipe, 11
Boar Meatloaf, 125
Bob's Venison Stew, 178
Bracchioli in Tomato and White
    Wine Sauce, 82
Bullwinkle Taco Salad, 111
Burger Bundles, 65

C

Cajun Antelope Steaks, 113
Cajun Deer Steaks, 84
Caribou Goulash (Bou Gou), 106
Caribou Tamales, 24
Charlie's Special Venison Meat Balls, 76
Cheesy Tomato Venison Steak, 73
Chef Eric's Poached Quail in
    Vegetable Broth, 172
Cherokee Casserole, 25
Cherry Dump Camp Cobbler, 154
Craig's Camp Chili, 108
Cranberry Venison Meatballs, 55
Cream Soup Rabbit, 135

Creole Venison Roast, 61
Crockpot Smoked Game Roast, 101
Crockpot Venison Ribs, 72
Crockpot Venison Tips, 85
Crunchy Cottontail, 182

D

Dan's Delicious Pheasant, 17
Dan's Primo Duck and Goose, 17
Dave's Famous Venison Kabobs, 18
David's Deer Stir-Fry Over Rice, 70
Deep Fried Pheasant with Dunking Sauce, 146
Deer Bar-B-Que Meatballs, 81
Deer Fondue, 84
Deer Fries, 73
Deer Roast, 76
Delicious Duck, 185
Delicious Venison Burgers, 35
Dick's Venison Jerky, 55
Dick's Venison Roast, 42
Dijon and Wine Rabbit, 136
Don's Totally Awesome Venison Chile, 57
Don's Venison Jerky, 37
Dove and Dumplings, 149
Dove Kabob Teriyaki, 176
Duck un Kraut, 165
Duck with Oyster Sauce, 169
Ducks on the Pond, 161

E

Easiest (and Best) of All Venison Recipes, 180
Easy Steak Marinade, 67
Easy Venison Roast and Gravy, 62
Easy Venison Steaks, 30
Elk Stew, 97
Elk Swiss Steak, 94
Elk Tenderloins, 107

F

Fajitas Texas Style, 60
Ferguson Stew, 96
Foiled Onion Steak, 51

188

Fried Squirrel, 137
Fried Venison Liver, 30

G

Game and Tongue Soup, 127
Goat Sauerbraten, 128
Golden Goose, 164
Goose Kabobs, 162
Goose Ravioli, 156
Gourmet Big Game, 96
Gramma Larson's Golden Goose, 19
Grandpa's Snapper Soup, 130
Green Chili Stew, 63
Grilled Antelope, 119
Grilled Antelope Steaks, 126
Grilled Buffalo Tongue, 102
Grilled Canadian Goose, 157
Grilled Duck Breasts with Red Currant
    Sauce, 160
Grilled Grouse, 25
Grilled Quail with Hot Sauce, 26
Grilled Southwestern Quail Supreme, 149
Grilled Venison Chops, 176
Grilled Venison Marinade, 65
Grilled Venison Steaks Lawry's, 175
Groundhawg Bake, 22
Grouse and Wild Rice Salad, 23
Grouse with Lime, 148

H

Heart Healthy Fajitas, 180
Hickory Sticks Mountain Lion Sausage
    Meatballs, 98
Hoppin' John, 28
Hot Stuff Chili, 74
Husker Roast Duck, 168

I

Instant Gander, 20
Italian Venison, 31

J

Javelina Loin with Mushroom and Pine
    Nut Sauce, 177
Javelina Mexicali, 112
Jess's Deer Chili, 32
Jiffy Teriyaki Steak, 64
Jill's Crumby Venison, 49
Joe's All Purpose Marinade, 66
Joe's Fried Venison, 52

K

Kabobs, 88
Kenny's Microwave Meatloaf, 42
Kent's Hot Deer Jerky, 79
Kevin's Easy Venison Jerky, 38
Kevin's Rabbit Stew, 130

L

Lazy Day Venison Lasagna, 68
Lemon Pepper and Pineapple Quail, 174

M

Madison Deer Loaf, 47
Madison Stroganoff, 46
Marinated Bear Steaks
    with Wine, 120
Marinated Caribou Strips, 110
Marinated Goose Breast, 157
Marinated Grilled Moose Steaks, 113
Marinated Mountain Goat Steaks, 99
Marinated Roast Venison, 39
Mexican Rabbit, 134
Mexican Venison Casserole, 39
Mike's Bold Venison Jerky, 43
Mike's Roast Goose, 167
"Mission Impossible" Duck or Goose, 173
Montana Surprise, 48
Moose Chili, 103
Moose Meatballs, 122
Moose Nose, 123
Moose Steaks in Mushroom Gravy, 103

INDEX

189

Moose Stew, 101
Moose Tongue, 123
Mr. Mac's Deep Fried Turkey Breasts, 152
Mule Deer Stroganoff, 44

N

Newfoundland Moose Pie, 112

O

Okie Roast Venison, 80
Onion Mushroom Venison Roast, 34
Oven Baked Bear Steaks, 102
Ozark Venison Roast, 43

P

Pacific Northwest Venison, 60
Partridge Supreme, 152
Perky Venison Jerky, 68
Pheasant Casserole, 145
Pheasant Diane, 16
Pheasant Fricassee, 140
Pheasant Goody Goody, 142
Pheasant in Mushroom Sauce, 14
Pheasant Jambalaya, 147
Pheasant Nibblers, 16
Pheasant Spread, 143
Pheasant Supreme, 147
Pheasant Tenders, 142
Pheasant Tetrazzini, 144
Pheasant with Wine Kraut, 145
Pickled Heart, 109
Pitica, 15
Porcupine Meatballs, 109

Q

Quail Brunch, 148
Quick Ground Venison Stroganoff, 32

R

Rabbit Dijon, 135
Rabbit with Gingersnaps, 133

Raccoon Patties, 138
Ram Arm Roast, 97
Randy's Whoo Chili, 81
Ray's Camp Stew, 80
Reed's Pheasant, 141
Rice Stuffed Wild Goose, 164
Ringneck Casserole, 153
Roast Boar with Polish Stuffing, 118
Roast Wild Goose, 163
Roast Wild Turkey, 151
Roasted Wild Duck, 179
Rocky Mountain Crockpot Roast, 41
Rocky Stew, 137
Rowdy's Teriyaki Pie, 105
Russ's Whiskey Wild Turkey, 13

S

Saucy Gameburger, 138
Sauteed Quail A La Marinade, 184
Seasoned Venison Stew, 69
Sheep and Cabbage, 114
Sheep Soup, 126
Shoulder Roast "Exotic Sheep," 115
Simple Big Game Corned Meat, 104
Skillet Venison Heart, 69
Slow Cooked Bear Stew, 117
Slow Cooked Pepper Venison Steak, 64
Slow Cooked Venison, 75
Smothered Baked Pheasant, 143
Southern Fried Armadillo, 131
Spiced Skewered Boar, 125
Spicy Deer Steak, 70
Spicy Venison Jerky, 33
Spicy Venison Sausage, 40
Squirrel Skillet Pie, 134
Stewed Venison Meatloaf, 41
Stir Fry Duck Breast, 184
Stir Frying is for the Bears, 116
Stuff Over Rice, 119
Stuffed Venison Steaks Ole!, 181
Sunday Venison and Raspberry Sauce, 77
Swedish Meatballs, 49
Sweet & Sour Snow Goose, 12

Sweet and Sour Venison Stew,
    Crockpot Style, 72
Sweet Roasted Rabbit, 27
Sweet-Sour Fillet of Duck, 165
Swiss Bliss Venison Steak, 59
Swiss Style Venison Steak, 75

T

Talbot's Famous Pheasant, 141
Tasty Venison Bologna, 44
Terri's Venison Stew, 78
Texas Venison Kabobs, 53
Turkey's Baked Groundhog, 133
Turtle Soup, 131

U

Upper Lightning Roasted Duck, 20

V

Venison & Asparagus with Brandy
    Mushroom Sauce, 58
Venison and Cider Stew, 67
Venison and Gravy, 45
Venison and Noodle Stew Mix, 63
Venison Barbecue Beans, 53
Venison Bologna, 31
Venison Burger Piroshkies, 71
Venison Burgers Deluxe, 54
Venison Cabbage Rolls, 86
Venison Goulash, 33
Venison Heart Casserole, 83
Venison in Sour Cream, 54
Venison Jerky, 74
Venison Liver and Onions, 36
Venison Marsala, 36
Venison Meat Pie, 35
Venison Meatball (Albondigas) Soup, 183
Venison Pancakes, 89
Venison Party Dip, 71
Venison Pasta Salad, 50
Venison Pepper Steak with Rice, 50
Venison Pot Pie, 52

Venison Pot Roast, 59
Venison Pozole, 61
Venison Shish Kabobs, 21
Venison Steak Brown Beer Soup, 91
Venison Steak in Mushroom Sauce, 57
Venison Steak with Onion, 34
Venison Stew, 37
Venison Stir Fry, 90
Venison Stroganoff, 89
Venison Swiss Steak in
    Sour Cream Gravy, 51
Venison Taco Salad, 173
Venison Tamale Pie, 46
Venison Tenderloins, 83
Venison Zucchini Boats, 90

W

West Virginia Venison Chili & Dumplings, 56
Wetzel's Venison Stew, 62
White Tail Texas Deer Chili, 85
Wild Boar Sloppy Joes, 124
Wild Burritos, 100
Wild Duck Gumbo, 159
Wild Ducks and Turnips, 158
Wild Game Barbecue Sauce, 20
Wild Garlic Duck, 168
Wild Goose Okie
    Style, 166
Wild Grouse, 153
Wild Indian Stew, 45
Wild Pig California
    Style, 95
Wild Rice Spanish Bake, 154
Wild Turkey Breast in Wine Sauce, 151
Wild Turkey with Sun-Dried Tomatoes
    and Pine Nuts, 150
Wyoming Venison Jerky, 79

Z

Zeman's Wild Duck Creole, 158

INDEX